Table of Contents

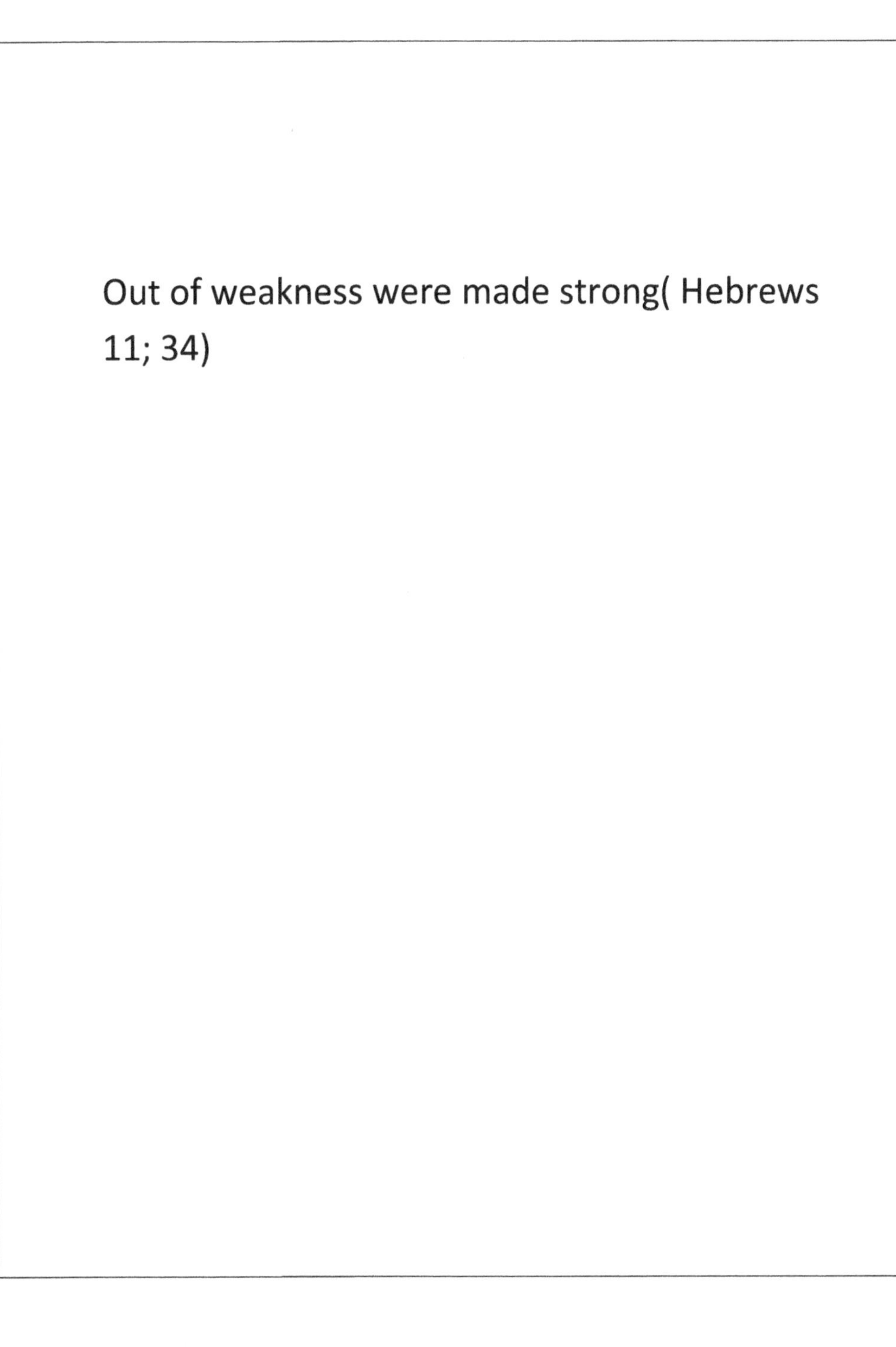

Out of weakness were made strong(Hebrews 11; 34)

INTRODUCTION

This book is not defining philosophy as a subject learned and taught in the universities, contrary to everybody's thinking, I am defining philosophy as the highest character dealing against the human mind playing different games against the human will by those who have mastered the art of twisting the minds of the unlearned common minds into every shape.

The reason that many can't stand on top of those who seem to possess some power, some strength, some authority in this life is all because those people on the other grounds have studied the human minds and have passed beyond the common knowledge.

It is the undeniable common sense that we are living in the times of highest knowledge of which are only those who have attained to it will survive or stands against the present and the coming worlds testing times. And to some points these results comes to us because at first we did not seek after knowledge instead we seek for the fertile lands to feed our flocks and plough the lands we possessed.

We grew up thinking that to be a man you have to know how to handle a hole at the field. That hunting for a lion and shave its beard proves you are a man. We invented a bow and an arrow and we stopped there, we did not wanted to trouble our minds for further discoveries, that for you to be a king in the African lands you have to possess all beautiful women in the village. We taught ourselves that to have many children means richness, forgetting that life demand knowledge.

The Europeans taught themselves that to be powerful you have to mistreat others, call them all bad names, segregate them, discriminate them and make them slaves, they were fools too when it comes to knowledge! For they didn't think about the future, they are the ones who taught us that the world is in spherical shape and that you always begin where you started from no matter the direction you choose to walk to explore the Earth yet the land of the dead they called it but her people are still surviving against all invasions.

And who taught the Americans that by disregarding the black community means to be a real American? And no matter how much your philosophy might be one should not forget that there is always some invisible powers that changes the times and the seasons of all human kind and what we think we know comes to be nothing but philosophy which makes us to look like fools in the future and that power alone is what makes the black community in America to sits in the honorable positions for nobody can stand against what the heavens have blessed no matter how much dirty you may look at it. You are a blessed land everyone admires and love you but," Has anything else good ever comes from the blacks?"

And you Africans who taught you that killing each other, hating one another, and being selfish from a brother make you a real African? You are a good land Africa, and you were fed the philosophy to believe that you are a dark continent, made you to believe that there is nothing good in you. And you think shading the blood of a brother will make you strong, how do you want to darken the light, which has shown in you? Do you think making a living by injustice will make you to survive and restore your honor? What philosophy is that?

Being it hard to ride over the elephants back, the small animals cries are never be heard on the ground.

Being it the handwriting of personal struggle against the human philosophy, this is the most exciting and inspirational rhythmic book that everybody must read in the world which have moved beyond the walls of the classroom time to get there, time to move higher. This will be part of your discovery beginning to realize that every step was designed to show who you are. You will not find your identity until you pass the path of the unknown end. Gradually you begging to find the good that is in you, something, which makes your pages and each step, was made to live a legacy for you. You are the best person with much in you the person the world has never have and the one most expected for the survival of many. Our duty is one, to do what we come here to do and this assignment is in every body.

There will be judgments coming from either side over your assignment the mountains so high and hard to climb the valleys so wide and dark in full silence where the only sound heard will be that of your own footsteps but unless you realize that your footsteps are leaving the footprints in that impassable path you won't be stopped.

You will not be surrounded by heroes or strong men you will need in times of trouble. Nevertheless the real you is a conqueror. It doesn't take a short time for men to believe and accept what you are doing, after all do not expect me to believe in you just go on because not everybody has got a bright eye and everything new in the midst of ordinary men who are used to what they know only, is received with much questions, nevertheless, everything good, overcomes.

Welcome to the decline of the human philosophy.

FORWARD

Life is a sacred and must be lived to the maximum. I wake up and turn my phones light on took my pen and not book which always lay next to my bed and write these words.

They were true words I read in one of the books from my home library; the wonder to me was that the person telling me those words in that dream was my father.

Ten years had passed without seeing him while I was in a strange land and while in the process of him coming to see me in a strange land he died two weeks before, I did not attended his burial ceremony and one week latter while checking my notes I come through this note book which I wrote seven years ago on that night.

And I knew there was no turning, no giving up, not even lost my hopes back to fight against the human philosophy.

I shook off all the challenges and thoughts, which underlet my mind and began anew, and the last words I spoke to myself was that; "I must live to the maximum." No more regrets, no more digging about the past, no more worrying of who did this or who did that for there is always the new beginning when men decides.

The biggest challenge we face in life is to forget how one has been fighting and conqueror some battles back in the days.

There are some memories of conquest and overcoming over big events in the past but amazingly, we come in a time when we feel like we cannot do it anymore we believed in big things then but time comes when we do not see it anymore.

We see ourselves as losers and defeated hopeless down and with the dark future actually the future without hope.

We become fearful people and we lost all the boldness we had and worse enough we change the language; we get the defeated tunes and we dance in them by praising some men who seem to be higher in life yet doing ourselves wrong by forgetting ourselves.

Yes forgetting; forgetting that we have big dreams to work upon and it becomes very sympathetic where we reached now when we take away our eyes from ourselves and began thinking that someone somewhere is capable of doing it.

We have not yet taught and there are no such lessons at school especially in our African curriculum of looking at ones potential before introduced to books.

I believe books should be there to compliment and modify what is already in someone than what is not there! If someone is, tough books should edify his toughness on how that toughness can help such person be introduced to the leadership and management books!

Unfortunately, we take courses and carriers we will not work in life and jobs we will not find. I loved English literature at school, and at home, I gathered to myself my own small library. Every book, which belongs to my father, I took it and when I borrow a book, I could not return it.

English literature students were scorned because were few and could not reach even ten, so everybody thought it was a useless and worst of time because reading about Ngugi wa Thiong'o's book "This Time Tomorrow" to some seems nothing but forgetting that patience and endurance is the potential of life.

That you don't just reach to the Mars without taking time to build the space ship and that you don't go forward without first looking back to find out what has been holding the future from happening.

ACKNOWLEDGEMENT

For so long I wanted to come to you brothers but time of the destiny has kept me away. This is the only gift I prepared for you,' To Terece Storey (and the Storey's family you are so dear to me) my bond friend. You helped my mother when I could not reach her you mean more than you think to me. My mountain friend Raymond Malikula(and the Malikula brothers) you never gave up of me when distance kept us away, you always kept on asking me when I would be back home. To my teen hood friend Dave Chipa Chirwa, without you I would have given up, you told me one to achieve one thing at a time. We lost each other on 20th January 2010 and we come to meet each other on the same date on 20thfeb 2022 and you come at a right time. To my mentor Nixon N. Issangya (now with the Lord) you are the one who told me that Iam a writer thus back ten years ago. All I have to tell you now is that "Now I write books." My young brother Wesley thanks for your unfailing love. To my brother Milton Ziwoya I break the silence now can't forget you brother how many times you come to my side when I needed somebody in that little time we knew each other seems a hundred years. All you did is still recorded in my mind brother. To Elton Cock my friend when I gave you this book to edit in 2017 you said "But I don't see it Declining" but now you agree. You have been so amazing. Time would be short to remember my iod time school friends (you will get yourself inside) brothers, sisters, friends, and all who will read this book you are so dear to me. Your time to read this book is so appreciated.

To all who love the truth, who fight for justice, who love resistance, patience and endurance, critics, exposition, mysteries, discoveries and light, this is the book gifted to you. Ones you take one page you will not be able to let it down so, fix your time well. The past, the present and the future is right here. This is the book you have been wa

ted to read for past ages.

Love you all.

THE DECLINE OF THE HUMAN PHILOSOPHY

Destiny on trial

xiii

DETICATED TO A MOTHER WHO DID NOT SEE HER SON FOR 12 YEARS. SHE DID NOT GIVE UP ON HER SON.

UNDER THE MANGO TREE

We were informed that any day the school regional education inspector might visit our school. It was not anew news; I used to see them in my early primary school level at Catholic Institute, and in short, we just called it C.I. In those days, we could see a change from our teachers one or two weeks before the inspection.

The teaching and the follow up on each pupil exercise book was faster and careful than before. In those days, we got clear education on topics we did not understood in the past but now they were clearly explained. This was to make each pupil understood and we could understand yes. Sometimes wish they could be serious always like those few weeks. "I was so young, but I could detect flattery."

What the teachers could do was revising the same topics; nobody knew what their goal was. All that love and openness to us was to flatter the inspector when he comes to inspect.

I remember our class two was under the two twin mango trees, one to the right and one to the left, sitting on stones as our desks, and running to hide in the corridor when the rainfalls but it was better because it was warm there.

And loving to place my sitting stone at the back of that outside mango tree classroom means not that I was a fool like what other teachers thinks.

It is truly the nature of some teachers to discriminate pupils, those they think are good in their upstairs are most of the times chosen to sit on the front line.

And the ignorant ones at the back making noise in their base vocals and worse enough are the ones in whose everyday's punishment falls upon. They are not considered as able but failures should teachers be happy to have pupils that he calls failures'.

All ideas men come to believe are purposed in one goal, and that is to turn people's minds positive or negative and both religion and politics targets to catch people's minds from the lowest to the highest or either way round. For I have seen under the sun that even slaves have got under them their fellow slaves who they command.

I just saw the big smile on the inspectors face, to my examination; he was impressed by the pupils' performance. That was it, my class three teachers had won the inspectors heart, and their philosophy had won the game. Two weeks later, I did not see them in my classroom. They had been ranked to upper classes. Now we had new teachers of whom I did not see the difference from the past.

What was happening when the school got the report of being visited by the regional school inspector was that every teacher including the head teacher could get their things on order so that when the inspector comes to inspect should find everything to be okay.

Should find that almost every learner in the class is able to answer the questions including those at the back without the inspectors knowledge that the pupils have just been feed the philosophy to recite the class lessons but when he turns his back from where he comes from, the pupils remains empty and receive sticks as usual.

They have just been used to lift those teachers to their wishes and after the inspector is gone, they start to treat us the way they want. Sometimes with their angry faces upon us almost to call us fools.

I believe in resistance, yes decisive resistance even when I know that what I am resisting against is difficult to win, and thus what gotten me that hush punishment years letter.

When your fellow boys recognize that you do not have a brother to protect you at school they take you as a banana tree that they can fly kicks and brows whenever they want.

I was not such a coward, my brother Justin was not with me in my primary school level. I had my sister Gertrude who was in her class seven while I was in my class three. I would be as a fool to run to my sister for help when I challenged the big boys at school.

Sometimes I would accept those kicks but not all the time and when the kicks become too tough to resist, I would frighten them that I was going to tell for them to my brother and those who knew I had no brother around, could laugh and add me another kick, and brows.

I grow up alone though I had my brother Justin I had never brought him any complains that somebody had beaten me and I needed his power to support my revenge. Not to him, my sister, nor my parents, I was independent of myself against whatever. I won some battles and I failed some battles too, but I moved on.

THE INTERROGATION

My form two head teacher come in the class one morning telling us to get prepared because an inspector was visiting our school the following day

Now that we were in high school level, the format was different from that of junior level. We were told to collect the data of all the challenges we were facing including all the goods and the bad so that we present them to the school inspector. We organized ourselves and put together all the bad and goods but the staff did not know that if there were some bad we would have gone that far.

Our main agenda was about Sir Benjamin our Social Studies teacher. We all agreed that we were not understand; not his subject, but his way of teaching was so poor, whenever he enters into the class all we felt was sleeping. Therefore, we made to explain it to the inspector.

On that day, I made myself as if I did not exist in that class. I exchanged the sits with my fellow and I choose the backline right at the very corner.

The fellows we choose to present our goods and the bad to the inspector were the ones we took to be brain fires in the class subjects. My heart was pumping abnormally during the presentation time and if my class representatives had left aside all other problems and speak only about Sir Benjamin, I would not have a problem with them instead, they did the opposite.

If you have ever seen clever men, then meet them in the moment when a tough decision has to be made then you will have a good time to differentiate between the classroom and outside the classroom. In addition, I come to learn that others have the wisdom, which has its boundaries around the school campus, and it cannot move beyond the walls of the classroom and that's the reason why they can't even serve their countries with confidence when they come to the outside world where they have to have only two vocabularies in the service for their people, "yes", where it must be yes, and "no", where it must be no.

But it's not their fault because nobody is there to teach them about good service only that teachers are there to teach them to have papers of class subjects which they call certificates and the Degrees to help them to have enough food and much drinks to expands their berries but become cowards when it comes to defend the truth.

I come to learn that we only go to school in order to have papers which will help the world to accept us, yes with our Degrees and the P.H.Ds, we become the most victimized people, and what we were taught as studying hard proves nothing in the world which has moved beyond the walls of the classroom. I was called by Sir Magombo to follow him to the staffroom and thus what I was expecting because the class monitor was the one who was called first and I knew I will be the next.

But the class was as quit as the sea. Others were laying themselves flat on their desks, few were whispering to each other, and I sensed soothing from the faces of my fellows they seem to be frightened almost to shiver and I knew what it was all about.

During the moment when our representatives were explaining the challenges to the inspector, the representatives omitted something from the report.

I knew this would be done but what pained me was that they did that without telling some of us and I think there was a certain group in the class which did it by themselves without informing some of us and that was a big mistake because we had already sat down and took Sir Benjamin's agenda as the first and most of all. They got afraid to speak about Sir Benjamin because of the fear of the punishments. But the good side was that the presentation was not done by writing but by speaking and the inspector could take notes himself. The inspector heard our concerns and before he checked out, he gave the chance to each one in the class to add anything if ever something was still a challenge. It was as if he knew the waywardness of my class representatives. And I knew that these are the moments taken only by the risk takers and not the fear takers. Everybody was silent though I knew this was a silent of fear.

After he repeated to ask us if there was something missing in the report, I stood up without raising my hand. 'If you remained silent in the day of oppression it means you are standing on the opposing side.'

And while you do not have much power to overcome the giants, and your mouth has not been shut, speak so that history should write your words when your breath has been taken away because of fighting for justice and those words will walk with your spirit to fulfill your task in the hearts of the generations to come.

I had no much to say, I directed all my voice to Sir Benjamin has left aside agenda. The inspector raised a question, which the answer was, "yes," by the whole class. He wrote it on his notes book and checked out of the class immediately to the office without asking for another addition. My call to the staff room was not of surprise but what I wondered was that I was called few minutes after the school inspector had checked out from the school. And if I was wrong, why not call me in front of the inspector?

I kept quiet to ask the staff this question, which surrounds me in their angry faces to interrogate me. I kept quiet even to answer the simplest questions they were asking me. The main question of my interrogators was why I told the inspector that Sir Benjamin is not skilled in his teaching. That was my Judasizim my interrogators wanted to eradicate in me.

Their faces had no pity over the truth and their hearts had no mercy over their fluttery. It means you know how to talk in the whole school isn't it? 'If I didn't know how to talk I wouldn't have talked.

Those were the same childish questions Jesus Christ kept quiet for and I kept quiet too. He told them he is the Son of the living God not only in words but also through miracles and wonders yet they kept on abusing him by claiming to be the Son of living God until they crucified him on Calvary.

Sometimes quietness gives clear answers to your accusers than opening your mouth. What I know is that I talked and I did not know the rest! Then one teacher raised a question, which seems to make sense. "Do you not know that he has a family to care about, do you want him to be expert from the job?" On this question I wished I had an ability to break apart my silence within me then I would have released an answer which would turn them all back like the thin Vietnamese did to the Americans in 1975.

But I like the Americans because they only talk of their victories and the big challenges they forget them in the grave of life. My answer would be what if we fell in his subject because of his poor skills and what about our parents who pay the school fees? My interrogators thought only to their side but not in balance to our side.

We have some poor parents who walk on the sunny day many miles on foot only to seek the school fees for their sons and daughters. Do they know how much sweat is sacrificed to get that little money? Yet, when we delay to pay it they chase us out of their classes and when they get it in their pockets they think it's time to dance and jock with us on the blackboard feeding us only philosophy.

THE BETRIYAL

Almost in every creature, there is philosophical nature. I have seen that every creature has its own philosophy in order to survive.

My son Prince when he was just a child of six months I detected a certain character in him of which I knew he was using his mind and not childish as her mother red it. When he needs something or sucking from his mother, he used to cry loudly until you give him what he need then he kept quiet. Has a child have a mind? Yes!

I tried to tell his mother that that was not normal but she could not understand until five years later. I told her he would grow up with that character she insisted he would stop. I tell you that it took some whips to eradicate that behavior even when he reached five.

It took whips war to eradicate his childish philosophy from him and I even taught him one day. 'Just go for the truth my son, don't go round making empty loud voices like our politicians do.'

"There is nothing to lose to go for the truth my son" Our politicians and religious men uses sight and words to caught the senses of men but you don't need the philosophy of words to a woman who uses her philosophy of wearing her miniskirt in order to deal with a man whose his senses have not been taught to resist against the temptations.

Prostitutes use sight to catch the stupid birds in their tiny suits. The birds, which go for every food, they saw without knowing what is behind the ground. Thus sight and hear are the greatest weapon of philosophy. How many good dreaming girls have fallen backward in the streets of Africa just because of lust for chips? How many beautiful marriages have broken apart just because of betrayal? Fake kisses, and dead I love you's, fake smiles, and deceiving hags.

I should say that our fore fathers fought well this worm called philosophy though they claimed no paper of education. They just used their common sense to discern between the truth and fake.

In the days of slavery, it was very difficult for the slave traders to invade some of the African places. They were strong in themselves that others accepted no retreat. They show their opponents the African weapon, 'the bow, and the arrow.' Hadn't it been because of some selfish and glutton Africans who decided to be tray their own fellow Africans to the Europeans it wouldn't be easy for the invaders to break Africa for such massacre of slavery. Europeans knowing the strength of Africa they knew they couldn't win by gun power so they entered in their books and read the philosophy which would make things easy than using much power to something which need not such a high power to win it.

Therefore, they took out from their books the philosophy of betrayal. They knew its snare would catch some Africans. "Let's do something, a plan which will make the Africans to betray each other, by that way; we can do the business easily."

Yes, their philosophy worked, they found some chiefs whom they vaccinated this philosophy by sight touch and hear. But I do not judge the Europeans for the loss and damage slavery did to Africa. It was all our ancestors fault.

The Europeans deepened their dream of slavery after when they found a clack in the hearts of some chiefs who by any means regretted not to betray their own people and brothers and sisters including putting to the map the bad history of their generation.

Slavery spread not by the Europeans, much contribution of the rise of it was done by the Africans themselves who through selfish gave in their generation to the hands of suffering. For the Europeans did not come by the way of force they used people and through them they did what they want. And this spirit is still eating Africa up to now! There is betrayal everywhere, from family members to church members up to the office members, the government leadership to a house girl and the houseboy down to the gardener. The spirit of wanting the high positions and fame without caring who will die or are bruised is seen even in the most trusted men around.

Any effort one may try to get his freedom shall always be lost if not mixed with knowledge. And humanity must be pressed before everything for gold and money cannot buy the lost breath.

Our time was the time of politicians and religious leaders full of philosophy. Since the departure of the Europeans in 1960s, in most of the African countries, those who sit on power showed no truth. Are few African leaders who are so rare to born in every generation; Nyerere, Kwame and Mandela and some few leaders who loved their people, and after them, many African countries have experienced the climax of negative political philosophy.

It pains many Africans that despite of having much and abundant resources Africa remains to be as poor as a poor man ought to be. Those in power are the ones be befitting from these rich resources. This would be the time for the Africans to forget the pains of slavery and swim in the happiness of her richness. Thanks to some leaders who have began to see the need of fairness in the happiness of African resources like John Pombe Magufuli the fifth president of Tanzania. I write that he will stand-alone in the current African history and those who did not understand him then, they shall after his death. attractive philosophy, the redemption of our tomorrow stays somewhere beyond their words.

A lie will not stop to be a lie, only that when the truth has been lightened it is when the lie stays behind. But don't think so that the coming of the truth is all victory, one should not cerebrate by thinking that by finding the truth then they have conquered the whole world. Ones one finds the truth thus the beginning of more afflictions than when you knew nothing and your oppressors would know it too. Thus, when and where the war begins because some people do not want to be seen and be known, all they want is to reign in the world of dead living human beings.

That was all the reason why my headmaster gave me such a harsh punishment by the scandal of telling the truth to the school inspector. I did not count these whips but they were landing in my hands with a commotion of a whirlwind and ends with an echoer in my hands. Next, was to mope in that big hall all alone, adding from that I turned to be an enemy of Sir Benjamin and no matter how much I tried in his subject, he ends up making me fail to make me regret of my foolish action All in all I loved him because that my foolish resistance made him to change his teaching format and everybody could understand him now; no wonder I passed his subject with a good marks during the national form two examination.

Poverty shall not go by riots in the streets nor fighting for natural resources for the whole history of the human liberty shows that all progress have been born out of struggle if there is no struggle there is no progress.

Those who preface to favor freedom and yet agitation are men who wants crops without plowing the ground. They want rain without thunder and lightning. They want the ocean without its awful roar of its many waters.

And no matter how long we may wait in the mouth of our politicians. No matter much, we may hope in their

The war between those who claim to find the truth and those who twist the truth for their own benefit shall continue and the suffering of those who claim the truth shall increase but at last, the truth shall prevail even in death. For the world has from the beginning live because of some few unfearful men who gave their lives for the survival of many.

KEEP QUIET.

("Sometimes people rebel because justice is not done." President Jakaya Kikwete the forth president of Tanzania)

When Rev John Chilembwe rose up a revolutionary to oppose the whites during colonialism in his country Nyasaland now Malawi in the year 1915 he said; " Lets fight and maybe our blood shall mean something someday ". Those were such a few men the world has ever gifted with, who saw life beyond death, which didn't sit in a problem and began to cry, men who knew that though now are limited in their physical strength, yet they may live for their tomorrow by their sacrifice. No wonder they remain to be men of all times and give the true meaning of what a man ought to be.

Today we call them fathers, heroes, freedom fighters, but many of them did not even enjoy the freedom they were for, yet, in their same affliction, they were still living in their tomorrow in you and me. But not all men are such so brave, it takes men who finds the truth and never think of selling it for any challenged prize.

Philosophy has the power to silence the truth and thus what I come to wittiness in my generation. the mouth of those claiming to know something over their opponents were kept shut and if you try to answer your bosses you could serve an innocent punishment and almost ending up in jail if not losing that your little breath, how lucky you are.

After the whole class head that I was whipped and given the punishment. Everybody left me alone. I remember sitting alone in that back sit desk. Nobody wanted me nor be seen getting close because of fear of being suspected to be one of me. I was abandoned and even the most trusted followers where no more to be seen.

But should we keep quiet over unrighteousness because of fear of being abandoned by the most loved ones? Standing for the truth is the path of danger and those who join that troop must be ready to be left alone on the Iceland of loneliness and must be ready to carry their own crosses.

These were my fellow students we agree together to raise our concern to the inspector. They were afraid and I did it, now when things came hot they all run away. No wonder we have the generation with fathers who run way from their wives and children. We have leaders who cannot eat vegetables with the poor on the same plate. The generation, which cannot stand in the hot, it does not want to suffer.

I remember how we used to be in form one. We were the same group coming from form one nobody got missing. One day while in form one, we just decided to lock the door not allowing any teacher to enter our class. We all sat on our desks reading our notes. The teacher came, but we had all agreed that nobody will go to open the door and if anybody dares to do so, we declare to show him or her slaps unforgettable.

We had no real reason of doing this but the most amazing thing was that we all stand on our decision unregretful. Our foolishness was that we did not agree on what to do when the punishment comes. The teacher went back and called the headmaster. He was Mr. Njiwa the same one who punished me in form two.

He came on the window commanding one to open the door and he did. None of us had the concrete reason of why we closed the door. Mr. Njiwa loved to walk with his office keys and every moment you meet him, you will notice him fast by his keys in his hands and as usual he had it on this day and now we had to learn the hidden secret behind the keys.

On the keys there was on it something like a nail cater. He touched it with his two fingers going round desk after desk line after line piecing it in whatever the part of the body he felt on the back, on the arms, on the lap, on the shoulders, all you could feel was the pain but looking in his hands you could not see the weapon. One could feel as if a scorpion is stinging him. He repeated doing the same three times but we all kept quiet and nobody tried to answer his question of who closed the door?

Those who could not endure the pain began to sob, while some of us like Suzika, we like to call him Amjiba or Tata. Diamond we like to call him Angoni, Zulieti nicknamed Alonda because of his big boots, Philip Nyirenda, Msawawa and Tintin I myself nicknamed Majabwada because of my fatness in those days, all of us our eyes were as dry as of a cat which is punished for stealing the fishes in the pot.

We refused to mention the ringleader and we all shared the punishment. Now in grade two I began to wonder, when my fellows did began to fear however, the answer I got that in grade one high school we had no idea of what the punishment would be. It seems that everybody regretted on that form one punishment. It seems that that punishment I and my fellows got in form one left some scars in them not yet healed and it comes back to life in form two, who wants the pain again though this was a different matter!

Nevertheless, what we do not know is that our children will come to suffer the consequences of unrighteousness we did not solve in our times when we do not stand on our positions.

You are in that department, you know of all the evils going on, but you can't speak out because you fear to lose your bread in the waters but I tell you that you will be the next if you stay quiet and you are the most evil than the evil that is done in the dark because whosoever cannot defend the righteousness is a killer and you are the killer and your children shall be deceived too for it will be well to him who remember to stand for the weak for the mighty God shall remember him and his seed in the times of the Jobs in exchange by sex, money by blood of the innocent, taking advantage over the poor and the unlearned, catch away the orphan's inheritance and eating what belonged to the poor and twisting the truth with a lie by their own advantage, yet, you want me to keep quiet?

THE BIRTH OF THE TRUE MEN.

I come to wittiness it; our time was the most untrue period the world has ever lived but somebody said that you can deceive the people but you can't deceive them all the times, and if you choose to stay on the liars side remind those your fellow liars to keep the records of all their lie because one day they must be reminded of what they said when the truth comes to take its place.

Men must not live to think that true men will not born they are the men who don't born in many generations but when they manifest they bring the wakeup call and even the past loses done by the wicked are restored.

Nobody under the sun needs a liar, even the liars themselves do not need someone to lie against them, and those who cause pain too others do not need someone to cause pain over them. Men's greatest duty is to overcome evil and all wickedness and it is not easy since we live in the world where the truth is changed into a lie where all evils have been painted all beautiful colors.

The battle may be as strong as beyond our strength but we are called there and it is our duty. Moreover, the first responsibility we have is to be true. To be true is our responsibility we must put on in this battle of fighting against wickedness and rise up justice to the throne.

Though we had been affected by slavery and then claim our liberty as free men, that freedom means nothing until today because there is no truth in our leaders both in politics and religious one.

I have met much people in my life who said that our fathers were not like us. I answer them yes. When I was a little boy I thought that big people never do mistakes and almost every big man told me that he used to be number one at school but when I grew up I learn that many of them didn't even step in class one.

The trumpet of the birth of true men must be sounded, how much strength is gathered, when we look back and look at the true men who born in the past generations. Thus it, it is to ring the bell of wakeup call in your time and resurrect your brain into the wise memories of which may be used to complete the duty we have in our time.

However, these were the heroes who had the truth and without pretending. President J.F. Kennedy was an American young man but which class do you put him, a young man? No! He was a father. Nelson Mandela started his title of being a father way back in his youth. Am talking of a person in whose there is the steps of a true man such are put into the line of being crowned a title of a father for one can be a young man but having big things in him beyond his age.

A true person always backs into the side of wisdom and brave. Never intimidated nor shaken. He always goes for the truth because he is the truth himself. Only when you are true is when you can be able to expose the hidden foxes in the caves, which hide to spoil the tender grapes in the vineyard.

Yes, foxes. I mean men of philosophy they are like ants they eat slowly under the roots and you will never know until the whole plant falls down but the truth digs deep down there and pull out the roots.

Who was Martin Luther the protestant? Yes, I go for men who establish their own footsteps out of the majority and become the real threats.

He is one of the influential true men in history. He began his protestant reformation in the 16 th century. The truth is that he was a truth seeker his truth thirsty lead him into questioning much about the tenets of the Roman Catholic. Am not here to tell you about Luther, instead I am talking about true men.

His father did everything possible for his dear son to become a lawyer; however, in July 1505, Luther had a life changing experience that set him on a new course. The thing is that truth seekers are not moved by time and the surrounding and are not lead. They can turn in every direction at any course. They are like the ocean. Luther decides to become a Roman monk the decision that disappointed his father but he felt he must keep a promise of himself.

Some men are men pleasers'; they think they can please everyone. Truth seekers are the most disappointing men you have ever met. They do not go for everything. They do not dance every song. They do not read everything nor watch everything. They do not talk to everybody and not every time. Their eyes are programmed their ears are governed by the discipline laws and their mouth is controlled to speak only on special matters and when they appear on public they are there to give someone a hope and comfort. For if, men cannot give hope to the hopeless and courage to the falling ones, then our presence in this world is nothing.

These are the men who born for people and die for people. They are the risky men who choose the pit of fire rather than the bowing down to the gods. They are excluded from the common knowledge because they believe on things which are outside this world like the South African boys and girls who sang" Freedom is coming tomorrow," but the most amazing thing is that at that time there was no hope of the freedom they were singing for; and unto the ears of the whites who were controlling them, their songs sounds crazy in the white's ears.

Such men, who can sing the invisible freedom on top of the world while in bondage and imprisonment, belong to the class of their own. They do not live a life of decorations with many tittles and most of all they will not be one of your choices. You want see them in the patties for their celebration and happiness is in the solitary places.

On October 31st1517, Martin Luther nailed a sheet of papers with 95 theses on the university's chapel door. By the end of two weeks, the copies had spread all over Europe and the truth began to be exposed.

No matter how much power may sit on the throne things must change. I do not rule that neither Martin nor the Pope were right, that belongs to GOD. What we look is what history has done.

How many transformations would be taken if true men would stand and show what they are, men who learned the art of returning the physical slap into a spiritual slap, who know that no happiness comes without its cost. The words of true men have legacy, they never die, and the oppressors have to hear them in their ears even when they try to kill them and erase them on the face of the Earth.

Men who choose to take the hard way have nothing to disappoint them for they live by their spirits. They revenge no one, they blame nobody, they hate nobody and the regret nothing because they mastered their will and they do not wait for men's approval when it comes to defend and stand for the truth.

We delay great missions because we wait for men to approve us right. Mind you that you cannot be either wrong or be bad when what you stand for is the truth. We wait for men to decide for us thus the reason why up until today, African countries cannot stand on their own. Not that they cannot stand on their own but that an African thing and whatever comes out of Africa cannot be proved right without the Europeans nor the Americans to be of useful internationally.

Even our own Mount Kilimanjaro, the Chaga tribe lived in that region for many centuries. They were the first to climb that mountain before the European explores knew that there was in this world a continent called Africa and before Columbus was born, yet, they wrote in their books by crediting themselves that Hans Meyer the German was the first to reach the summit of Mount Kilimanjaro in 1889 but the most amazing thing is that he had African backup the two local headsmen who guided him the way and if these locals knew the way how did they come to know the way if they had not climbed that way before! And why history is not talking about them? The Chagas were climbing that mountain to offer sacrifices to their gods long ago. My question is, were they not people to be recorded in the book of world record as the first people to climb and discover that mountain of their land?

They were not wrong to give the first rank to themselves but the reality is that we were taken as slaves and we were under colonialism and education had not yet reached to them to enlighten them to defend their rights to what belongs to them because no African has ever claimed anything in the European soil nor the American soil and now that we have learned and have known and the Americans and the Europeans themselves have taught us about our rights, don't we have the right to claim our African names in our famous places? Can our names not be there now since you have taught us about our rights? A procrastination prince will always gives the way of the king's throne to the slave's son and in turn he shall no more be called a slave but a master and the prince shall turn to be a slave. If you cannot value what you have, others will give it valuable names and even when you call it yours, you have already lost the honor while it belongs to you. I believe this is one of the fool shiest errors Africans did; to lost honor of her famous natural places in her own land.

We have Lake Victoria in Tanzania named after queen Victoria of England, we have

We wait for the approval from the donors the West and the international agencies to tell us that we cannot make it without signing dirty agreements, which are a curse to the gods of our land Africa. Our fathers did nothing by themselves without first consulting the gods of their ancestors and let to know what they say about the land. Politics and any other education nor philosophy cannot stand on top of the rules of the gods of the land and the sin Africans did is to take for granted the tears and blood our freedom fighters sacrificed to redeem this land of waling to the land of light and happiness.

If we had known the coast it took for Africa to be where it is today, we could not just give in to anybody as easy as we do today. We are like children who worst the inheritance left for them by their father just because they are not aware how much sweat and blood falls down to seek those riches.

And African gods cannot stay quiet when its children are doing foolish things, but wore to him who causes one of these little ones to sin. For whosoever wishes his friend bad times he himself shall not be safe.

The question is, don't we have true men in our time? When something belongs to you, you fear nothing in use of it. Prostitutes are the most confidential creatures. Who can speak badly of their nakedness? They expose the very same thing everybody calls it a shame, their big strength is in the very same shameful thing and with it a day cannot pass without catching a stupid bird. Do you think they sell their bodies? No!

They have found the secret and the philosophy hidden from their nakedness and have no problem to expose it knowing there are unlearned birds outside there that goes for everything. You have no reason to hide even when nobody understands you. I tell you that they get out from their rooms being confident of what their secret doors have assured their hearts.

True men are made in solitary confinement, you want see them today and the world may think they have not born yet. And none may realize their importance in the society. They are there. They are as if the C.I.A. only goes for the important national matters. Long preparation is the game they love to play before meeting their intruders. They are confident of getting out with the best.

Are those solitary places where they get the truth? Their school is invisible and you want tell where they get all these because their lives cannot be red in their teachers books. Their lives do not stand on their papers but beyond everybody's surroundings, thus why they fear nothing to expose the truth when time comes.

You see, you cannot dress a prostitute and promise to marry her while you will not fulfill all her needs.

A PROSTITUTE OF TRUTH

So I become a prostitute, yes, and a prostitute of truth too and I expose my nakedness to you who has the opportunity to read this book. She has a memory so difficult to be rubbed off in one's mind, ones you see it you will struggle to eradicate in your mind. She knows how to torture you without lifting her hand against you. She is like a wind on the ocean, everything gets upside down.

I am a prostitute of truth, my truth will torture you too, your education has helped your stomach but has left you empty, and now I will fill it with something else. That position has just given you that fame but rotten inside of you. You are like a baobab tree fat outside but nothing inside. Whom are you pretending against?

You call us prostitute on a day light but calling us sweethearts in the dark. You speak against us in the platforms but we worry nothing about that for we know you pretend. You come to us in your expensive cars in the dark promising to leave your God given wife and marry us while you know you just want to use us.

The thing is, if a well-respected man wants to be ashamed he should try to use a prostitute without paying her. They know the emptiness and secrets of the best-respected men. I must say that prostitute gets rude when deceived.

I am talking to you call who yourself a religion man, my name is a prostitute. You promised to live a holly life and yet you crow around your comers' house in the dark, you find us again whom you were speaking against in your sermons on Sunday mornings. I know you have just come to use us in the dark but hurry up because the day light is near to come.

I have kept my quietness for so long. Many years have passed since you promised me to be your free woman. But you only think about your own. You only come to us in the dark, do what you do and go and wait for another dark to come out.

Today I will sock all your clothes in the waters and you won't go until the day lights appears then you have to walk naked like me on the day light. Do not plead with me. The time of the truth has come and you have to tell us what has been going on.

Yes, I witness it, the time came when Africans get tired of lien politicians. Just theologians preachers who practiced something outside their sermons and dirty celebrities who proved nothing with their celebrations. Even a child cannot be deceived fifty times, fifty years had passed since Africans gets their independence. The hope of success and better life after freedom strengthened each African weak born and lost hopes.

Since Ghana first got her independence in 1957, many African countries rose up with a hope of greatness over the pain of slavery. Those countries that were strong in military and politics like Tanganyika helped their fellow African who had not yet redeemed their nations like Tanzania to Mozambique and South Africa. But in all this great history of African liberation, there was one man who saw the future of Africa in colonialism.

In his speech in June 1975 in Chikolopola village in the district of Mtwara, President Julius kambarange Nyerere spoke something, which I could see it in my generation. He bases his speech preaching on true freedom. He spoke of the glutton African leaders who took their effort to chase the white for their own benefit and not for the common people. He commented on the first freedom African countries got but wondered that the battle for the freedom was not over.

There was another colonialism coming ahead, the new colonialism. He said people shall hope for better life they will not get. Only shall be eaten by the few. He ends up calling up for the gathering to fight against that new colonialism. And today I ask why did we chase the whites? It is better to be tortured by someone who does not know you than one who claims to love you and calls himself a brother.

Were the liars keeping the records of their lies? Even the philosophers' perceived that the time had come when it is very hard to deceive the poor uneducated African, during the general election; one could detect the new hearts not only in Africa but in many parts of the world as well.

Darkness was lost its way and the political and the religious philosophy began to decline.

We cannot live for such as much as many as fifty years without learning the truth, and I tell you that even when they had to be thousand years, the truth would triumph. Who knew that after 500 years there shall rise a generation which shall claim their land? The Portuguese colonized Mozambique for all those years without dreaming of another day that true men shall born and shall learn.

We had some politicians who just took their people as prostitutes and some religious men who eat their own frocks and bosses in the working places who just needed someone for the use without any right. Who promised the development, which does not exist, love that never shared and hope that never reached. The world's big leader's discussions on how to end wars, which broke in many parts of the world, proved nothing but philosophy which brides the people's minds, they were the same ones seeking for the same prostitutes in the dark.

They do not send their troop in those affected nations to offer true help but for their own benefits. In March 2011, Syrian government led by president Basher al Assad faced the greatest challenge when the protest erupted throughout the country. The Protestants demanded an end to the authoritarian practices of the Assad's régime.

The Americans help to cease the war and not long, the Russians did the same. Then the French, German, and England left alone the Turkish army. My question is, they are the same big nations, which fought against Adolf Hittra in the Second World War the war, which just ended for five solid years and why today they fail to help Syria while all the big nations in military were there?

They could end up that war just in one day. I do not think there is any truth going on. And the world must come into the point of truth and speak it out. Who are behind all these label groups like the Islamic state, Boko Haram ,Arcadia and many others? What about Sudan, Libya, Iraqi, Yemen. These are all the nations, which are rich in oil, who can go on looking for another answer? There is underground philosophy going on. And those prostitutes in the dark only know the truth about the underground from these men.

It was the time when most African leaders never want to step down from office. Many of them tried to change the constitution so to stay in power for the longevity they preferred though time was not allowing them to. We had past the whites' slavery now it was the battle on an African against an African. Nyereres prophecy was coming true.

Most citizens start to run away from their nations just go to find refuge in the hands of the old masters. The saddest period of man during the 21st century and any of them droned down into seas waters and nobody cried over their lives, it became normal to hear of their boats sunk while carrying a vast cloud of Africans.

I believe there were silent cries at the sea. Words of the dead, which nobody got, luck to record, nor write. Those silent cries at the sea were only head by the most high when the waves at the sea brought them before his throne. Yes words, because everybody who dies in trouble left the words you cannot stand to remember. They become so painful to remember. Those were dark and the saddest nights.

Amazingly, no African leader stood up openly to speak about the Africans who were drowning into the sea! Those people were desperate for better life and were nor sinners. Their deaths were not taken into serious and nobody cares but I must tell you that whether you take into serious about the human lives or not, they all belong to their creator. And even in those dark nights, he hears the whisper of their desperate cry for help as they fight against that cold deep waters of the sea trying to save their lives but to no avail against the cold and the snow.

There was every reason for a young man in my generation to give up of life. That which was affecting the outside world was much more inside.

Many young people were told to turn stones into bread. To kneel down under the masters feet for the quick offer of the worlds riches. Were the ones taken to the top of the pick and told to fall down on a condition of being offered a saving angel and in the midst of such struggle, no angel showed up.

I myself was a victim of my generation, though at times, I felt it lucky to born in this generation but at times, I regretted it. If you have never come into the situation of seeing no reason for living, it means you have never met troubles yet. I hoped and I gave up, I felled and I arise, I cried and wipe out the tears. I feared about life and worried. Sometimes I saw myself a fool and sometime a great man overall, I learned through them all.

Many young men migrated to other nations for want of better life. Countries, which will at list, offer them a little happiness. Some fresh foods on the table and one bottle of red wine than the local made breweries. These young men were thirsty for a change in their nations and upon not seeing them chose to try their luck on the other world and it was risky because even in those nations they run to, were not easily welcomed. Many died in the hands of the country owners were abused, forsaken, betrayed, and misused.

They wanted to rule themselves out from being called savages. There was no reason to go on with the same style of life, which seems to fall out of rhythm. It is very wrong to say that many young people lost hopes because of lack of jobs in their nations. Jobs were and are there many of them but not sufficient to everyday's needs. This is all because of the lack of knowledge of the good use of the rich resources Africa has.

Hard labor with less payment, only good for the owners, they are the ones digging Tanzanite underground in Tanzania, copper, in Zambia, gold, in South Africa. Oil in Nigeria, and Sudan just to mention a few but their lives cannot be compared to those who just wait outside.

And even if I could speak of the joy needed to lift up those weak souls, then, it would be the other way round. Those who seek joy in involving themselves in sexual relationships become the most victimized than all. Alcoholism and robbery, entertainments and freedom of young men had left them with scars and wounds' it was more of destruction than the freedom and happiness it offered.

My generation was dancing in all sources of entertainments. It was making sense. Their scandals headed on Social Medias signaled to me that even these celebrities are taking us nowhere. Their dancing's and nakedness on the screens moves to no pick. All their styles proved nothing to uplift my generation instead it turned to add the fire of destruction and the path of the lost, for wherever there is no good conduct demons laughs in happiness.

The standard expected to be offered by our celebrities proved to be a downfall. Drug addiction had weakened many visionary young men. Instead of the upliftment and joy drugs promised, it was the sorrows of rotting up in the prisons. They did not build up castles in the air as they dreamed; instead, they build them in prisons and hospitals, while others die young before their days.

Young women involved themselves in prostitution not by their will; others were forced by life's challenges as they were denied the right to education and our African customs, which do not give the inheritance to female genders. Wars, which broke out in many parts of Africa, gave some souls with no option for life. This led to many young people to make bad choices for before we judge it is good to know that not everybody gets the grace to help him at the very moment of his need. To others it takes long and others die before it reaches to them.

Nevertheless, the human will and spirit must not resigned in moments of crisis, it must go on looking for a solution, however; overwhelming the odds, you must not accept defeat, you must not believe your effort to be in vain if you have the blind courage to continue to endure and to struggle, there is always a new beginning in your life.

With the orange lights, which were shinning upon them, they were looking as Hindu girls. I am not that so much to get my eye's attention over women, I do not flash my eyes just to anything I see. Twelve hours had passed since I entered in this country. Since morning, I had not yet seen any women so beautiful like them, actuary I had forgotten if I had seen any. It was as if all people I see on my way were men.

One of them had long hair flashing down on her back, I like it. Her long nose with a small mouth made me to bring back the memories of home girls although years letter I came to have my wife in this country.

The other one had short hair with reddish like skin color. From the bus window, I noticed them as sisters of which in some minutes to come my imaginations were not deceiving me. Closer to them stood a man with dark skin and shining eyes," he looked handsome." They were all pointing their fingers to the bus I was in, lifting up their eyes up and down with their necks twisted here and there like flamingoes fisting on the foolish fishes.

Everybody was getting out of the bus, but I did not notice until I asked a conductor where we were. Since it was in the midst of the night, I had no idea of the place since it was my fist time to land in this nation. The conductor answered me with amazement. "Oh! We have arrived, this is the end of the journey are you Mr. Daniel? There are some people waiting for you outside there."

On the bus door, I lift up my eyes and I saw a hand waving at me, Wahoo! It was like an accident without effect. Two distant imaginations come to meet each other. There are situation in life where our minds leads us unto all the truth but we lack self obedient therefore, losing or left behind the luck which was forwarded directly to us and sometimes we even don't know how to treat our thoughts with respect.

Twelve hours ago, I experienced a miracle an expected. It was a miracle I pioneer it myself without my awareness. I had taken the evening bus from my national business city Blantyre going to Lilongwe the capital city, where the following day I board my next bus from Lilongwe to Mzuzu city the northern region. I took my calculations I knew I had started a new discovery of my hidden life, every step was much more important, and each step had to be recorded.

I met my teen hood friend in Mzuzu city in the morning of 20th, January 2010 Davie Chirwa. He had now completely changed. I examined him to be cool and focused, there are young men who recognize the times and know how to change with it. He had grown up not only physically but also more upstairs there. He had at least a nature of a man. Some good shaved belt and short hair in his descent trouser and a shirt. "He looked gentle."

I thought I would find him in our old life. Back in the days where we used to call ourselves; 'Yeomen' or Ma yooo! Those were the days an A African boy started to experience the western life. They are the years of 1990s when an African girl began to put on miniskirts. But the complete of an African culture took place in the years of 2000s.

Those who could not accept the modern life tried all their level best to establish strong rules against this type of dressing tying to bring back the old African type of dressing. And those who still believed that African culture could not be changed found themselves surrendering to their own born children. All the punishments promised by some leaders and parents to bring upon what they called rebellious children fall downward on their noises.

It becomes completely impossible to prevent a girl from putting on a trouser or a miniskirt, and as hard as removing a tooth from sharks mouth to prevent a young man not to loosen a trouser half of the buttocks. They look as if they have helped themselves in it.

My father's friend from abroad sent him some gifts and in it, I found in it a walkman with strong headphones. In those days we used cassettes Terence Story had a lot of them, that walkman did to us more than modern boys. We had nothing now but music. 50 cent and other American rappers were in fashion and though I was not good in memorizing songs as my fellow friends did but I was good at selecting good songs.

Music becomes our food wherever we went. We could boast ourselves in that walkman as we exchange each other in turns.

The most exciting moment was when it become Alexis Kumala's turn to put on the headphones, we liked his jumps up and downs putting himself in the flow of the music with all his hands twisted trying to rule himself from local boys and be an American boy in the African streets. It was time for an African boy to dance.

Every generation changes and must be talked with dressing and music when it becomes to young people. The new fashion had just come into the local markets. Boys took the American dressing style while girls took the European style. While my friends chose those big jinn trousers having a big sticker written 24 hours on the back and front, I did not run into it fast. I put myself in myself. My friend Alex had that 24-hour trouser jinn and such boys were called yeomen simply means celebrity life style. The movement in those jinn's was that of American celebrities especially the Rapp men.

In those days, all it could take for one to be like an American boy was one pair of snicker shoe, Nike or Adidas was in fashion. And if at all you sacrifice a lot, Timberland shoe, do much more honor. Those who want to go much far could put on big men necklaces and others tie a piece of white cloth on the left hand, putting on a cap written one of the American labels could add extra touch.

Having such appearance even without money in the pocket you could become girls dream.

It was a period where every style moved with music and many boys tried all their level best to boast their music for music systems like the smart radios we have today were not chipper in those days so we used creativity minds to boast our small radios to put ourselves into the world of noisy music. All one could do was to find something in a form of a drum, cut a round hole on top of it fit for a speaker you have. Place a speaker on that hole with a wire that goes to your radio, it was done. One passing by could thing you posses one of the smart radios because that drum made a lot of base.

Terence had many of such like drums so I took one and made myself a music star in my area. But when you reach to Alexis home it was all noisy, one could think it's a Hollywood.

The most beautiful thing was that we were addicted to nothing but fellowship. In our group, we drunk not, we smoke not; we fight not though we feared not the intruders only that we were good at coating girls. Though I was the shyest among the group, most coins head fall on my side only that I was not busy with them unlike my friend Terence who could not let go of the luck. And Alex was a silent killer nobody could know he took the coins when not everybody is around.

In the past boys fought over girls, they need but in the modern day's life, it is all up to you how you fix yourself and how your pocket speaks. For love is not interpreted in trust anymore, for in the past love was what gave the meaning of money but now money is what gives the meaning of love.

You have money in the present days you will get a woman you want even another man's wife who is not taught to be faithful who get men for their profits and not for love. And shame on you too men who betray your own God given beautiful wives.

Parents had no problem with us, going to Terence's home or to Alexis home were like going to another home. At school we were not that bad, we were kind of boys who when absent from school on that day one could feel that something was missing. We were the stars of making laughter and excitement, adding the feeling of love for existence that we were not born to groan and regret of life.

Thus how I interpret my past. I looked at that past that although we liked the American life and the western, and try to be like them, our hearts and identity as Africans cannot change and we shall always be Africans. There is no other better place in the world like Africa. We love all the people, all races, there is no black or white in Africa.

There is no hate, no separations, and no discrimination. We are beautiful and smart. Our character is not like that of the western, the love they sing is not the love they live, and if anybody preaches about Africa as a place of evil then ask yourself. We invented the arrows and the bow not for killing a fellow human being but for hunting and defense against wild dangerous animals. They were turned to be the enemy's weapon for the first time when the whites invaded our soil.

Then, we were taught many philosophies until we learn the courage of turning the hunting weapons to kill our fellow Africans. Betray and classes of living began there.

Show me the love you preach about and I will dance with you. Show me your arms wide open for the desperate and the lonely. Bring back the lonely world and I will be for you too. I tried to look forward at a time where an African boy will still stand on his identity and never swept away by western nor American culture. Yes, my wish happened but in a different style.

An African boy danced that American music, got addicted, and become worse than the American celebrities themselves. The western life misleads my generation and it had no way than to forget her identity. Drugs entered in our poor undeveloped countries and the philosophy, which was preached to them about the new generation, turned them into fishes. The nakedness, which was known by the Americans in their streets and screens, came to our African daughters. And that was the beginning of the mixed Africa and the decline of her culture.

He was no longer a boy in the group of boys singing cultural songs and tells the tales taught by elders sitting around the fire at night as the night blue sky gives a color to a full bright moon with one shining star close to it. He was no longer a boy sucking milk of the cow to eat with stiff porridge at the grazing field. He was no more a boy among elders making baskets and mart under the big tree drinking the African drinks put in a goad brought by respected girls covered himself or herself with kitenge or kanga.

Those were girls with nothing to lose. Self-respect among the society was their great lesson. Proper dressing was one of their virtues to get favor from their fathers gods and their gods were happy with them. Their gods protected them and there were no women diseases not even in their vocabulary. They build strong families focused on obedience and respect and such families stood as a lesson to the disobedient children.

And when the world talks about women empowerment and forgetting about teaching these women to focus on building strong happy families, I wonder what these organizations preach about. We have empowered women with money but without any happiness with troubled families. We have empowered women with high positions but divorced and separate family and the lost children. The preaching which goes on that says when a woman has money she can make a happy family has turned out to be a fake philosophy. In the past, those women had no money but they were happy and had able to stand on their place and the title of a mother had a meaning to them. Money and positions alone does not make a woman. But money, positions plus self-respect and good virtues makes a good mother.

African culture was based on building strong families with dignity and honor. Life without respect for one's self and others was considered inhuman. And these three lays a strong life foundation; respect, obedience, and trust. Africans trusted in their culture although I should say that there were some customs, which were not convenient like beating women, land, or property sharing, forbidding women to work, and castration of women. Those were the only customs, which were supposed to be omitted from the African culture, but the rest was fine.

When people change and erase their identity on the face of the earth, it means they are the people without a source. African marriages were praised for staying longer and dying young was considered a curse. They no longer grow up to be faithful mothers' fathers who had no vocabulary of divorce and separation. Respect between the young and the elders have lost its power and the elders, which were the teachers of good conduct in the society, are on the front teaching stupid behaviors to the young people. They are the ones in the prisons for the cases of raping and child abuse and marring teen agers.

Fathers sleeping with their own biological daughters as elder mothers take advantage over weak young men. They grow up to be celebration fathers and mothers sitting together with their children at the sitting room watching together naked celebrities on that big flat screen and the word sex, is not a secret vocabulary anymore.

Worse enough, some grandfathers, and grandmothers refuse respond to our African way of greeting, they want; "hi!" They are no more grandfathers who used to stand as a pillar correcting and cutting off any misbehavior before it goes further.

And the act of allowing her daughter wearing a half naked style in front of her; is unhidden truth that African grandmothers and grandfathers, mothers and fathers have been defeated by the present philosophy and her past foundation have been broken.

Our African culture was just the philosophy and not the truth because truth never changes but philosophy does. But the blind character of philosophy is that it can for many centauries stood and be trusted as the truth thus the reason why, many great people fall and history only remembers them as a shadow; which has no power to shine when the darkness comes.

I believe history must bring somebody alive and still use him in the present and the future. It is something, which Africans must erase in their memories that their culture shall come back or be used again in the future. It shall remain to be rich history but without use in the future. Western culture did not came to change African culture, they are the Africans' themselves who have changed everything.

The fist people to show new life to the Africans were the missionaries. They brought the culture of education and the subject of clothing did not start today. It is not true that the old missionaries recount African culture as dervish, and unwanted. One thing to remember is that these missionaries differ from many things for example the issue of clothing.

There were some missionaries who deprive Africans from wearing in the western cloths but on the other side, some missionaries encouraged some Africans to change their way of dressing and thus what some missionaries did in one of the area in Kenya. The Nandi tribe was wearing the goat's skins and necklaces. The missionaries told the Nandi to remove their clothes and necklaces for they were very dirty and had lice. They used to put on these clothes and necklaces' the whole arm and around their necks which made them to forget about bathing.

In the same way, goat's skins were very stinky because they put on oil to make it shine. Nandi's women were very stinky making other women not to associate with them in the church. And because of this, the missionaries advised the women of Nandi to stop their native wear but this was not necessary and the missionaries kept quiet on native dressing. As the time passes, the change comes itself for the Africans themselves saw the world which was changing and which needs the acceptance. It becomes so hard for them to on with their goats skins wear.

But to say the truth, the African natives lived inside life without any knowledge outside their environment. Despite it all they were very happy.

They began as missionaries writing and questioning about African culture and as the years passed, they come in the name of the anthropologist. Anthropologists are people who study about culture and way of life especially the tribe's way of life.

The anthropologist from America and Europe come to Africa to get the information of the culture and the customs of many African tribes. Upon my arrival in Tanzania, I found many of them walking around as they seek for the elders who know more about their tribes' culture and history.

Rev Nixon Issangya who was my host introduced one anthropologist to us. We were introduced that they are looking for these information for the sake of writing thesis for their college university studies but though I had many questions about them by then I had no answer. All we were told was that they are students who want to complete their studies nothing more.

These anthropologists enter into African interior and found a Masai, Meru, Chaga, Kikuyu, or Lomwe.

They began to question about culture and customs of such like tribes as they took notes or recording and after they finish they fry off home and compile books about Africa and way of life and when an African needs the same information he bought it from them, but thus not my point, let them sell it and publish it on the internet.

My question is: how can we buy our own knowledge from the strangers? And what shall happen in the future when there shall born another African generation, which shall want to write about their culture and way of life? They shall have nothing to write about because the Europeans and the Americans had plundered all the information.

As of the year, 2012 an anthropologist employed in the United States repotted an average hourly wage of 28. 95 dollars and salary of 60.230, according to the Bureau statistics. The lowest paid 10 percent of 16.02 dollars or less while the highest paid 10 percent made of 43.82 dollars or more. Those employed by the federal government received the highest wage in 1021 of 35.60 dollars an hour.

Those working in museums and other historical sites earn 30.37 dollars an hour. And those who do scientific research and development firms employed more anthropologist than any other type of employers and paid an average of 26.87 an hour. In 2016, 7,600 people were employed in US as anthropologists.

Who is powerful, the one having knowledge or the one having history? It is better for one to cut off your heard and go with it than one take away knowledge from you, because the one having the knowledge about you has your weakness too and has the power to control you too.

Thus why it seems that Africa has got nothing of its own because all knowledge had been given away free while they fry back to be paid a lot of money deceiving us that they are just working for studies! Moreover, our fathers shall have to be answerable for giving away such a rich inheritance without thinking of their children. How possible they see their own culture and customs as useless that they did not see it useful to their children's

Amazingly, some of the people interviewed were educated enough. a 60 years Director from the Macmillan school was interviewed on June 24. 2015 by some Russians. A 38 years old Regional commissioner for health from Tengeru was interviewed on 24th, June 2015. A 76-year-old pastor from the Usa River was interviewed on June 8, 2015. I got these ones because I thought they are living in the new generation therefore they have much knowledge of what is happening in our days than those our grandfathers who were interviewed in the past! Is this really a dark continent with its people pretending to live in the light without knowing they live in the darkness of their minds?

Those who send those anthropologists are big and rich organizations like the institute of Ethnology and Anthropology, Russian Academy of Science, Moscow State University, American University, and The Association of the Black Anthropologist etc.

And if those who come in Africa to correct data are paid, then it means that those bosses make a lot of money upon getting the information because some of the data are used to teach other Anthropologist studying in their universities.

Some Russians interviewed a 77 years old poor farmer in 2015; I do not know how much that poor father was given anything!

MEETING A MYSTERIOUS DRUNKERED

I met a young man in the bus during my travel from Mzuzu city in Malawi to Tanzania. The bus had taken its route in Mzuzu at around eleven pm night and reaches the Malawi Tanzania boarder Songwe at around five am. The gate of my next destiny was seen few steps ahead of me. A young police officer searched us before getting out of the bus. I get out, and the first thing I had to do was to go straight and touch that gate and speak some words of faith to myself.

I then enter inside the immigration office and present my travel documents. It took almost an hour for all of us to get documents checked up.

I head men speaking in unknown language. They were selling water a distance from the main gate. Maji!, Maji! They were holding 500ml bottles of water in their hands. I read on the bottle was written Kilimanjaro but I failed to connect my brain between the picture on the bottle and the words. We entered the Tanzania territory few minutes letter. After register our documents again on the Tanzanian side, the bus took off to Mbeya city.

Some people drop off on the way so there were some empty sits on the bus. I decide to change a sit and choose the one close to the door because I needed some fresh air and guidance from the conductor since it was my fist travel to Tanzania.

And to everybody who travels across the boarders knows what I am talking about. And on that sit, I felt comfortable with my book but little did I know the reason why many passengers avoided that sit. I come to notice that almost four people sit on that sit soon moved to another sit. I took a sit and care for nothing and I did not even care to look who is my neighbor I continue reading my book as if nobody exist in that bus.

To my surprise, I took notice that others were whispering as they point to the young man who was sitting next to me. I do not either remember what happen but I found myself stand up. Then while standing, someone catch my book from my hand. Thus when I realize that I had taken a sit together with a drunkard thus the reason why many avoided that sit. He was deadly drunkard never even aware of himself.

Lucky enough he knew English and upon reading the back cover of that book he raised a question to me and he wanted some more clarification of what he had just red. He was badly stinking but I found myself give myself in to this young man. I sat close to him I began to explain to him according to his question. In a minute, I made a friendship with him but it was as if everybody in the bus was looking to see my endurance to something, which everybody had resigned and if at all I will not give up and thinks of changing a sit like some did.

We talked for some time and from nowhere he disappeared from the sleep. He could not balance himself so he staggered while sitting sleep. I fear he could fall so I tried to hold him back whenever he loses balance. It was a big job. I head others shouting from all corners of the bus "Live him alone and fall to break his head on the floor so that he may learn the badness of drinking!" I did not know why but those sounds increased my love for this young drunkard.

I knew him not. I had never even met him anywhere in this continent, he was not a Malawian. And I even not knew his name or where he was going. The only information I had was that he was a Tanzanian and since he was coming from Malawi, I knew he was going home. I squeeze myself to him and place his head on my lap. There on my lap he felt at home, he went away in deep sleep, and I took his phone from his hand and keep it.

In just seconds, all my clothes were stinking and it was hard to breathe but I regretted not for thus what I chose. Any kindness has no regret and any sacrifice does not have to be remembered.

When your inside assures you of victory in the choice you made, do not resign even when the last person you trusted most stepped aside and left you alone in the midst of a thick jungle where the only voice coming inside of you says you can't make it all alone. Those are the times when your lonely strength gets challenged and the last answer you give to yourself is to prove that the majority were right.

As I sat there looking at him I come into my visual eye. We live in the world, which has given over the young people, and many of them have been left alone in their choices and nobody cares. I made a quick calculation of the fathers, mothers, aunts, and uncles and parents in that bus who wished the destruction of this young man. They had better see him break his head than seeing him exist safely. I said to myself; how many young people of the same kind they have in their nation, community, and homes?

So I said, then, they wish for the destruction of many. I saw the different world where the weak cannot be strengthened and the failures cannot be given the second chance. Where sinners cannot be pardoned and the wrong must die. This is the battle every generation must face and I saw no difference from the days of tooth for tooth and eye for an eye, where the righteous must face the consequences of their righteousness and the sinners must face the punishments for their sins without anyone to face their punishment instead of them.

We arrived in Mbeya city at around 10am in the morning. My host who was in Arusha city the northern part of Tanzania had sent the money to Mr. Munisi his friend residing in Mbeya to buy my bus ticket to Arusha the next morning and I had to sleep at his home but upon calling Mr. Munisi, he told me he was in Dar el salaam city by that time. Since I was not familiar with the new environment I stood outside the bus wondering what will happen to me with the fact that Mr. Munisi sent to nobody to welcome me if at all he knew of my trip why going empty without sending anyone in his stead? I was dumb.

While standing there with questions without answers I could never know what was happening to the other side. Meanwhile many passengers had come out of the bus except some few whom I notice that there was something wrong inside. I walk towards the bus door only to find that some people were knelling down looking under the sits as if something was missing. It is when I saw that drunkard young man. My mind told me that he was seeking for his phone and I was right. The phone was with me and he forgot it.

I called him and he stepped towards the door, "a phone?" I asked him, before he answered I showed him. He could not believe it, now all his memories came back and he realized he was fully drunk some hours ago and he sat with someone he never knew but the most amazing thing was that all along, he holds my book in his hand but he could not know he holds a book in his hand until he saw me. He just smiled back and he turned back and told everybody in the bus that it was over! He found it. I just saw some women pointing fingers at me and others showed to be surprised. He told me letter that those people were just wondering what type of a person I am coz if it was somebody he could have gone away with it.

He soon made friendship with me and he asked me about my next destiny. I told him of my situation that Mr. Munisi who was to host me in Mbeya was away and he did not send even a representative. He tried to call Mr. Munisi himself from his phone but the network was bad so he told me not to get worried. "I will take care of it just be cool," he told me. By this time, his Uncle who was a taxi driver came to pick him up home.

This is the same young man others wished his dearth some hours ago, yet, someone was waiting to pick him home.

His uncle was in hurry but he cooled him down after explaining to him my situation he then challenged his uncle that he was to go nowhere without me and told him he couldn't live me alone until he make sure I'm safe. His uncle intervened and he said he knows somebody who owns a restaurant and a guesthouse by the same name and maybe he might be a relative of Mr. Munusi, we drove off.

The young man had promised me that if he will not be a relative of Mr. Monist he would take me to his father because he saw that his father loves people of my kind. We sat on the back sit and there we had some secret conversations. So amazing, he told me he was a son of a pastor. My father is a pastor and he will love to host you and take care of your next trip. So worry out! He went on telling me of his hidden life. He told me that he does not know what is going on with him after all being the son of a pastor he felt to betray his father and God. He told me he was not like that but he found himself falling to this world. I understood him with inside ear, for we are living in the times where many young people needs quick riches and in seeking for those riches the cost to find it becomes higher than their papers sometimes and in giving up they found themselves bruised and broken.

Those falliers gather in them anger and violent and turnout to be rebellious against the world and blame everybody around them as a cause for their going through. They blame the government and all leaders, parents and everybody. But when a goat or a cow falls into the pit every effort if taken to pick it out, then why the effort to save our fallen young people seems to dilly? Although our generation seem to walk away from the real life, yet, it could come back if it could find a still small voice the problem is that everybody is angry with them so who will be a friend?

I looked at him, he spoke with passion, then the shouts and wishes of those passengers in the bus ring again in my mind,' we are killing this generation alive because we don't have the time to listen to our young people. Do not judge someone to condemnation before listening to him. Not all young women prostitute themselves because they wanted it! Many of them were betrayed. They were promised the promises, which did not existed, and some house girls they run way from the bosses' abuses and denied payments.

Others are orphans, all their properties were taken, and all parents died. Relatives took advantage and off no help to them. And today when you send police cars to catch them at night in the streets what are you doing! Why catching them without want to hear their stories behind and what made them to be like that? And the police patrol you sent, demands sex with them to set them free from the custody. They are the same police patrols who sex with them taking advantage over the weak. "He, who has never sinned, be the first to throw a stone." They are the same rich men who went along with them and you catch them to hide your sins.

We arrived at the restaurant, yes, he was Mr.Munisis blood brother. What a connection! Mr. Munisi's brother was the one now who made all effort to finish my destiny to Arusha city. Upon hearing of my visit to Arusha and that I was hosted by his brother he got very happy and soon made connections with Mr.Munisi and I was greatly honored. I got everything I needed. I ate what I needed and sleep in his quest house in a double bed room with fresh air all because I loved a drunkard young man.

It was in the beautiful afternoon while sitting on the restaurants verandah that I remembered that young man."O! My book,' I yelled to myself. The young man had gone away with it and I regretted not. "Thus my gift for you for all kindness you did to me, you become my angel. Remember me through that book wherever you are." I said those words to myself facing my eyes to the sky. And I believed the massage was sent by the invisible spirits. We never met again and as I write seven years have passed but I am looking forward to meet him in whatever the world, perfect and true.

During 1400s, slavery existed; African slaves start to appear in Italy, Spain, France, and Portugal in 1442. In 441 European slaves, trading in Africa began. The Portuguese captain Antao Goncalves and Nuno Tristao captured 12 Africans in Cabo Branco (Modern Mauritania) and takes them to Portugal as slaves.

In 1691, the captive slaves from Africa first landed in northern America at Jamestown Virginia. Racism started during those years and mostly between the whites and black. Racism has been there for generation after the whites come to know there exist people with black color but the blacks did not do the same to the whites! And it is amazing that the roots of racism had not been cut off from the face of the earth and it seems that a time will come back where racism will take its power again in the future.

The abolition of slave trade in 1808 in America shows the decline of human philosophy, which for many years shows that nobody, can stand above it. It is good to remember that racism did not yet finish. The fact that some white Americans are still abusing the black community like what happened to George Floyd, it's the clear evidence and proof that the roots of racism are still on the grounds and they are strong indeed that the black community will not breathe in the future and if the gods will not send another Martin Luther king; there shall be welling days.

The early African Kingdoms were much advanced similar to that of European Kingdom. A Dutch reporter in 1602 on the West African kingdoms of Benin said the town seems to be very great when you enter it. You go into a great broad street not paved, which seems to be seven or eight times broader than the streets in Amsterdam. The houses in the town stand in good order close and even with the other as the houses in Holland stands.

One traveler described the inhabitants of the Guinea Coast around 1680 as "very civil and good natured people easy to be dealt with." "Do what Europeans require of them in a civil way are very ready to return double the presents we make of them. Africa had a kind of governance like Europe based on Agriculture and with leaders of lords and vassals. European travelers in the sixteenth century were impressed with the African Kingdoms of Timbuktu and Mali already stable and organized at a time when Europeans states were just beginning to develop into the modern nations.

In 1563, Ramusio secretary to the rulers in Venice wrote to the Italian merchants; "let them go and do business with the king of Timbuktu and Mali and there is no doubt that they will be well received with their ships and goods and treated well and granted the favor they will ask. I cannot stand to believe that African development was surpassing that of Europeans. Someone has to born with much confidence who can say; "tell those foxes that today we are rebuilding our Africa and tomorrow we shall be perfected."

Our fathers did all that great development without technology we have today. They were able only by using their pure minds. And today, who has bewitched us to underrate ourselves that we cannot make it? Many observers held Africa to be a lost cause purely based on climate, which was blamed for the mistreatment of the local population by the colonial powers. In an article in the March 1910 issue of the Atlantic Monthly, James M. Hubbard referred Africa as a land in which no white man can live for any length of time and retain his faculties in a normal condition.

Prejudice towards Africa was just as strong in the United States as in Europe, and was related to the virulent racism in American society towards its own black citizens especially in the South. It had taken the United States longer time to do away with racism than Europe. How could black children study along whites? Henry Garret who was the head of the psychology department at Columbia University wrote. The black African has no written language; no numerals; no calendars or system of measurement. They have not device a plough or a wheel nor did he domesticate an animal; the only thing they have managed to do is to build nothing more complex than a mud hut or thatched stockade.

Negative stereotypes of blacks were presented to generations of the American schoolchildren in their mostly segregated classrooms. The story of African continent was presented with a wrong face in America and Europe. Africa. The fact that most stereotypes written way back in 1898 offending Africa are still remain on the list of recommended standard on the American children's books is a clear proof that racism in America will not die.

The most notorious offender was The Story of Little Black Sambo, written by Helen Bennerman, an Englishwoman living in India. She describe the black child as lazy, slow, and stupid loyal to his white master but liable to lie and steal and violence. American firms in 1950s and 60s released firms showing Africa as a place of bad spirits and idol worshipers showing a native boy who wear fetishes around their necks and attack white women at the slightest opportunity.

The effort of Africa to attract American attention has been there for more than two centuries especially during late 1950s and early 1960s, when independence began to command the world scene but Africa has been unable to help to focus American attention. This has been so due to Americans view about Africa that they can't trust whatever comes out of it and if not be so President Donald Triumph would not be confident referring Africa as toilet. America is interested with the resources Africa have but is not interested with Africans.

Since the end of world war II Africa focused her eyes on America as her redemption for economic rise but thus not what Americans thought about Africa and until today Africans expectations from America has not come to pass. The tough demands of American funds upon Africa are the clear lessons that Africa will not get it easy as they imagined, and it will never be. Forced to sign dirty agreements of homosexual in return of funding shows the truth of how much American regards Africa as a trash.

But what should we say now? Should Africa continue to point her finger to America and Europe? It is foolish for any African born to point finger to America or Europe because of all the bad and lose they refer and did to Africa whether it be racism or slavery. It is even stupid to regret about slavery for the time is and shall be when the builders shall seek for the stone they rejected and despised.

It is time to cerebrate for we conquered the unbroken philosophies. And its time when history must come into light that all they believed about Africa was all wrong and it will be. The belief the Americans had; that a black man would not lead the white house got them wrong. The belief that Africans are monkeys was wrong philosophy for if a monkey can in the evolution of time chair the United Nations then we must ask ourselves; was that monkey clever or stupid? Kofi Annan would have answered this question better than all of us and if a monkey is able to lead the white house then Chares Darwin's philosophy about the evolution of man has a great advantage over the Africans.

Then, I do not have to argue about being called a monkey if a monkey has reached to that great height. And I do not have to argue about evolution beliefs if evolution has helped to change an African stereotype from a lazy, slow, and stupid black child to a great man in the White House.

There is a celebration somewhere in the spirit world and all must come into it. The spirits of those tortured by slavery and casted out by racism are watching. Yes, they are watching since 1950s when Africans began to regain their land independently. Watching in 1997 a black Kofi Annan chairing the big United Nations formed in 1948. Yes, they watched Mandela breaking down racism and apartheid in the African soil. What more the cerebration it has been when Obama step in the White house, it has to change its name now and be called the Black and White House, its philosophy name has declined.

Even the Asians were not considered as whites in the America and Europe thus why Banc Moon was raised so that no stereotype should remain to stand in history. What do you do when you win? You do nothing but to "Dance." Do not think so that the spirits of those suffered in slavery are sad, there is not even anger nor revenge in them. Dance in the African drums no more sadness, no more sorrows no more pain no more dancing on Bob Murray's "Buffalo Soldier reggae" yes; stolen from Africa to the White House and the United Nations.

A black boy seeking for survival in the streets of Chicago and Los Angels he found himself multiplied and stand in all talents from music, films, basketball and science. We have to dance together with them, they are watching in the angelic form. We do not have to remember slavery and racism in anger and hate instead we have to see it as victory to a Blackman, so come to the dance. No matter how much great you might be but if you fall at last your story matters no more.

TESTING MY FAITH

It was on the 25thof January 2010 the day, I arrived in my neighboring country Tanzania. The conductor pointed to me those people who attracted my attention before. I stepped out and they come closer with smiling faces. I shook hands with all of them and without many words; they led me to the car, which will take us home.

The elder sister of whose I came to know her by the name of Mercy, opened the left front door for me, I felt honored; nobody had ever done this to me. I knew I had been most welcomed though at the same time I had no idea of the challenges waiting ahead of me. She and her young sister took the back sits, I felt comfortable on my sit alone while I discipline myself not to twist my neck here and there like a village boy and as you know its natural in the persons having one thing in common to avoid looking each other's eyes and while men are confident enough to look in girls eyes but is not so with girls. Men can took one two seconds to look in the woman's eyes and in the next second throw a word upon her for men have got nothing to do with taking time want to know a woman's background or who she is, they follow their passions than a woman's story while most women need to know who this man is first.

The reason is that women are afraid of men's philosophy though at the end they are conquered by the same philosophy. Things have completely changed unlike the past. There were no such cheaper women one can have the very same minute you ask her prize. I heard from our elders that they could walk miles and days until the shoes hill is polarized just to seek for the "Yes" of a woman. But one could ask and say; why they were so such harsh and hard against men?

Should we say they had no desires like our girls have today? Didn't they not in want of money also like our present women? Did they have no passion for love as most of women expose their feeling for love in the social Medias today? What about the subject of our present generation of women of being confident enough to propose men in blue eyes without bricking? What magic were they used to keep themselves cool and look at men as hungry dogs?

Today's women are talking about women empowerment and giving them the chances and rights to do what men do. A woman has been strong all along and I don't know what they are talking about? Tell any woman in this world to remember her ancestors and she will come back to her strength. If you could ask me of who is a strong woman I will tell you that those in the past were stronger than our eggs and chips women we have today. Any woman, who knows and stands on her position in the family and the society, needs not to be preached about the empowerment. The problem is that we are empowering women who have lost their positions in the family, education, and the community thus why we have confused families all over the world!

The issue of young girls to get enough education is the only solution if the women themselves need to attain equal rights. For how can the competition be if they are not educated? Men have educated themselves and can stand on those higher positions and if women are not educated to that higher education how can they be equaled in those positions? We live in the times where only the strong in their minds shall stand, if women are not confident enough it will remain to be a story because nothing comes without strategies for how can women who ends in class seven be equaled in men. Positions and competition does not come without qualifications and if our women qualifies who can stop them? And shame on all countries, which put many hindrances to girls' education a matured and strong man test his ability by allowing others in the game.

And many men are weak today because of women who have lost their positions because when a woman lost her position, men struggles a lot to make it because God made it so that no matter what, all men will be incomplete without women on earth. It means falliers of men will be so great if women failed; because, there will be no men's helper. For what happiness is there for women to rank on the high positions, fame and worthy on earth but without a position in the family and without joy with her husband?

Grandmothers and mothers were standing as leaders to build strong and happy family. A woman was taken herself cursed if she did everything but and failed to bring happiness in the family. They believed in family happiness than silver and gold. Everything was done in focused on the family's happiness. They ate not fancy foods we have today! They ate boiled sweet potatoes sitting under the big mango tree with a jug of water and the sounds of laughter in loud voices was head some meters away.

Not fake laughter's we have today living in a fancy house with all the decorations in a round table with all the fast foods of all spices; unfortunately those spices have failed to bring the family's happiness in our present world because food does not goes to the stomach, it goes to the heart because without the happy heart food will not go to the stomach. Without a happy heart, those spices mean nothing.

Any woman having happy family will not lack development. They were hard on men because they believed themselves to be the best and they needed not men's approval to tell them what to do. The philosophy going on about equal rights will be a dream if the foundations have been broken. No woman can do better in her empowerment if left confused and unhappy families behind because money does not buy the family's happiness.

Girls who dream to grow up to that rain ball weeding surround us. All they dream is a weeding. They talk about entertainment not struggle for their future families. They think about the life they see in the screens and movies. They read about Romeo and Juliet and they think they will have such love in the blue sky. They dream about money and think about money as a family maker. We have families with much money but sad faces.

We drove off Arusha streets and in some minutes, we reached the residence. We came out of the car, Mercy and her young sister went in the house. I was left alone outside and it seems the door was closed. I kept my coolness. The first to show up on the door was mother and with faces alike, I did not want to be told who she was. She was Mercy's mother. She looked at me while touching one side of the door, up and down and after a minute of silent she break the silence and say words of welcome.

I knew why, because normally mothers who have their beautiful girls do not want to see handsome young men like me around. Every handsome young man is looked with a different eye. Mothers look them as wolves come to destroy the ripe grapes in the filled and every smart young man is received with precautions. And she looked at me to see whether I am a village boy or a town boy.

It is easy to discover a village boy. One is his footsteps, the movement itself can tell you. Two is his table manner, you will be dumb when give him town fast foods with all the town mixers. Three is his tongue, language pronunciation will tell you he comes from the village. Four is his neck. He twist his neck to everything , he wants to see all things at the same look and he wonders a lot about the environment you will regret to take him to the center of the town. Five is his talkative mood; he speaks so much even in the things he does not know he acts as if he already knows them all.

If you receive, a visitor and he seem not to rest his neck upon entering the house. He looks this, he looks that, just know he does not know much yet. Even some educated men and women go to Europe and America to wonder about things and worse enough they come back the same without even learning anything. They prove to be fools for even when asked about their countries they become dumb.

It was almost 8pm at night. I looked at them all; they were tired but not weak to entertain my presence. They asked me to take a shower, I did, and on my turn from the shower, my food was ready. I ate as if I was not hungry, I reduced my speed. I needed to eat as fast as I could because I had not eaten anything for 18 hours I drank only water. When you are a visitor do not eat like a hungry hyena cleaving for a dead elephants bones they will need you to go back as soon as possible. No matter how much hungry you might be, do not forget to left some food on the plate.

At last, they asked me to take a night prayer so everybody can go to rest. I did and Mercy escorted me to show me my room. We said goodbye to each other, she went back. I closed the door and enjoy myself a peaceful rest on the bed; I looked at that beautiful sailing board and closed my eyes. I said a little prayer and give myself a hope of a new beginning of another day in the foreign land.

" God, help me to overcome every challenge whispered by many voices that I can't make it, I know there is nothing easy without struggle but help me to conquer" without knowing I fall into sleep. I was awakened by a knock on the door without knowing but was already in the morning, I knew who she is and I was not wrong. I dress myself up and hurry out. “There is a young man waiting for you inside, he has been sent to take you to a place you will be staying.” It was not good news to me for I had already fall in love with this family but I had no choice, I had to move.

I brushed my teeth and went inside to meet the man, he was called Baraka. However, he could speak broken English but we could understand each other well. We took the breakfast and it was time to move.

I thanked Mercy’s mother. “Thank you for everything.” Learn to speak in short form; do not make a long list of everything, thus delaying time. We matched out; they all escorted us towards the gate. She closed the gate and continues to escort us. I looked back at that closed gate and that closed gate, marked the beginning of the unknown survival for struggle against human philosophy.

SILENT YEARS

Our philosophy has taught us to concentrate on education, making a lot of money, be famous, and live a rich life but it is all nothing to achieve all these if not surrounded by right people. We take many years to achieve our highest goals in life but we forget that whatever the achievement we may try to attain may not succeed if destructive men get along.

Untrusted men we met on this life's journey have cut down good and great visions. We do not just need friends but the right and the necessary friends. We do not just need people but the focused ones with strong ideas and active minds without it we gate lost in the silent world with visions and dreams in the mind. There are great young men out here but bad people have locked them down and cannot be exposed anymore. Destructive people without humanity full of jealousy and selfish who can't help to lift up somebody and worse enough they are discouragers of everything good and they do not believe in other people's best.

Destructors rather than builders, vampires and not makers surround us. We need politics which will bring the nation together and work together despite the difference of political parties, the day when African politics will mature and grow up for the benefit of the world. We cannot go on with this fighting and childish politics of killing each other after the general elections. The meaning of politics is not fighting and opposing you cannot be on the opposing party and oppose the development agendas in the parliament! There is no opposition party in America! Thus why during my life time following American politics I've never seen fighting after the elections because they believe in America than in one person so America is greater to them like any political party candidate. The money we have in African countries are funded money yet; we throw stones and destroy the little development we got by debts, we break shops and set fire the recourses we got through many sweating and tears just because of politics, do our minds working or we have been bewitched?

We need the religious, which will make the people and not just have them for the sake of offering. We need leaders who know that life is only lived ones and they must do their part with all the passion and love. Family is which will live for each other at all coast. Parents who will make the children and children who will make the better world. We need wives who will make good husbands and husbands who will make adorable wives in the society. We must stop to live entertainment life instead of real life.

I came to myself that I had not missed Mount Mulanje for I had here with me the great Mountain in Africa Mount Kilimanjaro. I had not missed rivers of home nor food; there are things, which can be similar in life but not people. A man having necessary people in life even when he goes away from his people and take his steps to the land of mountains and valleys, in desert and jungles and face testing times alone , yet; hope and strength rises when know he is not alone but he has loving and good people around though they might be afar.

To have a good friend is a treasurer's gift on this earth with has many deceiving fake smiles people. The best person who has lived his life here on earth in this short life is the one who struggle for people and make their lives better and make them to feel the warmth of being humans and not dogs, such people live their lives to the fullness and have nothing to lose when dearth approaches.

In life; friends must fight together and share the spoil equally, must wipe together and celebrate together. Therefore, my life was filled with such memories. Seven years had passed since my departure and resisting myself from memories was impossible but I had to make decisions.

Through my secret spy in the social medias and other people; life in my country was not such pleasing. The Kwacha money had declined tremendously, things had risen up beyond common people's pockets, and many young people had run away to South Africa to find jobs in the mines and companies. The political atmosphere was dark; the death of President Binguwa Munthalika in 2013 put the nation to the greater coast than before his death. His successor President Joyce Banda who comes into power because she was second president according to Malawi's constitution lacked wisdom to lead and on the general election in the same year, she did not pass.

She failed to have good relationship with her fellow neighboring countries like Tanzania and her agreement to sign the homosexual agreements for the sake of international especially the American funds made the gods of the land to deny her despite of making history as the second African woman to chair the president sit. Malawi is the land where righteousness lives, thus the reason why the court cancelled the 2019 general election, which gave Professor Peter Munthalika the brother of the late munthalika a win. But on voting again on 23rd ,June 2020, the opposition party won and Rev, Lazarus Chakwela from the opposing former Malawi Congress Party becomes the new Malawi President.

The justice revolution had been possible and from now on, I called that nation as; "The only land in Africa where justice revolution is possible." Because since the times of one party system one could not dream these changes could be possible in the land where people used to live in fear and torture. Little of these stories are not known by the outside nations but Kamuzu Bandas time was the most horrible times each Malawian who lived in those times cannot forget.

Kamuzu Bandas era was such a horrible and his down fall in 1992 was a great lesson to the generation to came that there shall never be al life president nor a president who will do what he pleases to do as long as true men gets born and learn.

It was 1991 still in my childhood when his party youth he spread all over the nation invade in our village. I do not remember whether the day was sunny with blue sky or dark and cloudy. It was his party's command that each Malawian should have a citizen identity card and if not without it the punishment was so severe for a jail was waiting for you.

Those who did not have the cards because they couldn't afford to pay its fee, the choice was one; to be alert to run on their bare feet when the party's youth appears or accept to be taken to jail of which others is not known if they could comeback safe. People were living as strangers in their own land and the freedom gotten in 1964 was just a shadow. Afflictions went on even after the British went back. It was the period of second tribulation coming from a brother.

The day has vivid memories of the sufferings I got lucky to witness. I just saw men running for their lives running towards the village cemetery to hide while others run down the river bushes and not much time I saw the youth party in their red uniform with angry faces with pang knives on their hands. Looking closely to them, others had carried sucks of maize on their backs of which I noticed that they had snatched things from other homes.

It was their usual character to take whatever they found at any home and nobody had the right to ask them anything since they called themselves Kamuzu's sons. They matched towards our home. My elder sister Thokozani had already coached me to tell them that my mother was not there in fact my mother was inside but seriously sick and unable to wake from the bed. One of them a tall one frightens me with a pang knife that I should reveal where my mother was. I stood on my resistance and told him boldly that I was not aware where she was.

For the third time their faces looked without pity, I began to cry, and crying was a big mistake I did. A mother who knows the pain of childbirth can resist herself to the sound of her child's cry even when she is weak to the last breath. In a small sound of voice, she tried to raise her voice to shout to the men to leave me alone and one of them head that sound. Thus when they discovered I had deceived them of my mother and they entered without hesitation.

They thought my mother was acting to sick in order to run away from the penalty of the card in fact my mother's identity card had expired its time limit and she had not yet had a new one and to them this was big lie because in Kamuzu Bandas era those who could not possess the identity cards were taken as rebellious people who are against him to make the revolution. Two strong men lifted her up from the bed but she could not stand since she was too week so they decide to drug her out like a suck of maize.

Coming outside she could not stand so she fall down and no voice could be head only sobbing from inside. I looked at those my fellow citizens who suffer their own blood Malawian in order to please someone on the throne, yet looking at them they benefit nothing because they were as poor as a poor man ought to be. They seem to enjoy the game. I took them to be poor not only physically but also mentally because they were supposed to realize the change needed to free their fellow citizens from the hell of afflictions from the selfish throne.

For how can a normal person with all his big and large head agree to go to afflict his own fellow men and this is what is happening now all over the world, the news of innocent men exploding themselves in the name of righteousness is the style of the day. Is one person on the throne more important than hundreds of children and mothers who die in one bomb explosion? Should we continue to make destructive actions for the sake of our parties? And what is wrong with those innocent bloods?

They had been fed the philosophy, which turns their minds to look at their fellow men as grasshoppers; and another one had to born to teach them look and see their fellow men as total humans and not dogs you can throw a stone at any appearance. Philosophy will teach you that others are better than others are while humanity will teach you that there is neither upper third nor lower third, no white or black. There is neither superior nor inferior we all born to help each other cross the broken bridge of life.

My grandfather who comes from nowhere was the one who help to save my mother from these unmerciful men. Kamuzu Banda himself was not bad but his people make him bad enough. In his time, he encouraged agriculture and I do not think so he could tell his people to work hard on farming in order to plunder their crops in turn. He was not aware of all the filthy things his followers were doing and they hide on his back to do what they want.

As I ponder upon that past, I fall to believe these were my fellow Malawians. The struggle to free you from the oppressions coming from a brother is the biggest fight we have today. The struggle may be a normal one, it may be physical, or both normal and physical but it must be a struggle for power has nothing without a demand, it never did and it never will. We need the actions and decisions, which shall never make us, regret even in the struggling times. The standard and stillness, which shall never find us, tempted, to seek the same prostitutes in the dark.

BACK TO THE MASTERS

One grandfather who was keeping his beautiful bird said to it one day; this is your freedom day, I have stayed with you for so long. He took it by his hand and said to it; fry on your wings, go and never come back; there is everything you need in every direction you will fry to. But the poor bird comes back on the following day seeking for its usual place where its plate was placed for food.

The old father saw it and said to it;" what brought you back here?"So he took it with much anger, breaks its one wing, and told it to fry but it couldn't the poor bird keep on cycling on one place because one wing cannot change the law of frying. At last, the poor bird begs his old master to fix its wing of which it took much time for it to be healed. Thus, what is happening now; all African countries fix their eyes on the Americans and the Europeans for their economic development and are not known when the true financial independence shall be achieved.

All African countries look for the economic healing outside their environment and despite of the rich resources they have, still they do not know what to do because if they had known what to do they couldn't go back to their masters to beg for everything even the most smallest things they could do by themselves.

MY CHILDHOOD MEMORIES

I grew up as a village boy feeding my grandfathers goats wearing a torn shot on the bat tacos and without a zip, running bare foot to the grazing filled chasing after that black female goat with long hones which always runs in front to invade in other people crops.

I hated it more than all the goats. I do not even remember the name we gave it.

Our clothes were as dirty as our skin and many times forget to bath in Chiwale river; worse enough; with all the tiresome of the day we could urinate on the sleep and I will not be true if I say I slept on the bed by that time.

We sleep on the mart and other families, which could not afford the mart, simplicity, was the way to survive, they could lay on sucks and cover themselves with sucks again, and life went on.

With dirty clothes smelling with urination, we could wake up the next day the same, taking the goats to the filled again.

I am sorry to say that the generation coming after us is will be the generations without experience and with no history of themselves because everything is made for them and they are there to use what others have already invented for them. They will be without personal stories of their childhood experience.

Today's children spend most of their times watching cartons on the screens and playing games on the computers and their parents phones. We were so creative in our foolish playing.

Our village had a river with clay soil on its banks. We could go there, dig the soil using our hands each one with its pile on his hand come back to my grandfathers veranda, which was cemented and began to mold cars of our dreams.

We mold different types of cars on the cemented ground though it was not all such easy to play there, my grandmother was so tough because she was the one moping but soon after she mops we turn again to mold and we got used to her but it was very sad after you have finished molding your dream car she hide for us and come unknowingly to break our cars and throw everything away warning us of not comeback of which, we turn in few hours to came.

Learning to build grass houses was one of our favorite hobbies. Each one could build his own and when possible go and attract girls to come and see and there began children's playing until late. Young girls learn to cook food at those playing and they could cook real food as boys run here and there doing their part making sure all goes well. Today's girls reaches twenty without knowing to cook perfect food, it wasn't so in our time and worse enough get married without knowing to cook perfectly because they are busy on the phones.

To possess nothing at present but see yourself from the worlds prospective shows what you are. There was a one hundred feet mountain at the back of our house in Blantyre. When I was young, I and a group of my friends could climb at it and stand tall. At the back of it there was a valley reaching to the river passing down it.

The small mountain had many rocks both big and small. During the holiday seasons, we climb up there and some few girls who were not intimidated. We loved to push those big rocks and left it rolling itself down into the river. It was so exciting to see the rocks rolling itself, as it hits against other rocks down the way. Then, with full force, splashing the waters, off it sunk into the deep waters forever to face the coldness and never come back again to the top. All we could do was to shout, making loud voices showing ourselves that we have triumphantly done the job. We could clap hands jump up and down celebrating the victory.

We went back home, the night comes and we covered ourselves in the blankets to feel the warmth's. I grew up and I come to realize how much torture we did to those rocks. To us it was a joyful game but to those rocks, it was the stupid joy.

Our greatest problem in this life is selfish. As long as our thing gets done, we feel okay never mind the opposite side. Our philosophy is to seek the joy and reach to our accomplishment never cares the wounded souls we meet on the way. It seems we live in the world where everybody is in the hurry, where the wounded must care for their own wounds and the dead must burry selves. The world where the rich must celebrate the presence of the poor and the strong rejoices for the existence of the weak.

From my childhood, we fell to see things in general. If the poor are not destroyed, the rich will not be rich and will never progress. We rush for one thing and forget the other. Sometimes we think like a cat, which was caught on a trap.

One grandfather who was keeping his fat and beautiful cat set a trap in his house to catch a big rat, which was destroying his grains. The grandfather's cat failed to catch this rat because it was so fat to the fact that it could not run across the wars to run against the rat. He put a big roasted fish on the trap, which smelled so nicely. The grandfather won the cat: "do not come near the trap!" and the man went in to sleep. In the midst of the night, the cat could not resist itself from the smell of the fish so it left its master on the bed and silently walk towards the trap.

The cat was caught and the effect was so big that in the morning it died. The grandfather said to it in tearful voice when he was burying it near his house; "you would have eaten both the fish and the rat if you had listened and waited, but now you have lost the fish, the rat, and your life too." The biggest mistake we do is to see ourselves children when others sees us big we go by the majorities judgments upon us and what men speaks is what we believe than what we see and know of ourselves. It is so amazing that when we were children we saw everything big, but when we grow up the world's philosophy deceives us and our understanding changes that we become so hard to believe in influential.

The strength and force to do something falls and we follow the laws and the rules to do what we believe while when we were children we asked nobody to go roll those rocks down though they were heavy and bigger than our strength but we could do it, everything was so simple to do and each one of my readers have your own childhood memories which has full of victories in them but when you grow up everything changed and can't take a stand to believe in influential. And the childhood force, which could do everything in us, dies by the worlds laws.

And if Africans had gone on with the same spirit to fight against slavery and independence and use it to seek the economic freedom, we would have been so far but now it seems we lost the first morale.

LIFE WITH A SOLDIER

The unforgettable period in my stay in the strange land was the life with a soldier. Too years had passed then I was introduced to this man by the Mission which hosted me for some years. His name was Mafie.

Mafia had resigned from the Tanzanian army for his own self-reasons and now he saved God at his village and since he was living alone by that time, I made a good company with him. Most of the times I loved to question him more about the army and the life he lived at that time. Living with him was all exiting.

He told me one day: some people cannot be put on the front line on the tough issues. Thus, what happens in the army. When the army is weak in front, no victory will be claimed. Not every soldier can be put on the frontline during the war. The battle goes backward when the frontline is weak and the opposite when the frontline is strong "Life is a war; he concluded."

Mafia made me to go on doing what I believed despite that I was against the time. He keep on reminds me that I was on the battle field and it was up to me to left for others to control my frontline or to stand myself, because living the frontline for others would be my choice but taking the binoculars and see myself and older the fire myself would be better than waiting for an order.

With Mafie, we did not live a sweet life. I meet him during his toughest time on his family issues. He was bankrupt. The house we lived with Mafie had a big sitting room with one bedroom, without electricity and at its roof was blessed with thousands of bats. They make a lot of nose at night throwing its feces on my bed, they bored me. The windows had no grasses making it to give me more coldness during the night.

By bed was on that sitting room close to the window. When the wind rain comes the drops of rain which finds its way through that empty window, could wet my bed. The floor had no cement but at least this gave me easy time than thinking of mopping all the time like the African pulps in the government schools

There was a kitchen outside the house, it had no roof, I could cook there using firewood and heated by the shining afternoon sun and go hungry when the heavy rains falls, and during one of the heavy rains, the back side wall of the kitchen fall flat that one passing by could see me fighting against the smock of fire forcing it to light as tears fall from my eyes because of the smock from the firewood which resist to light up.

I hate people especially women to see me cooking so I place back the bricks temporally because during the night we used the other corner of the kitchen as a bathroom. Inside the house was hot sometimes so when I wanted to refresh myself I could take my book and take a sit in that empty roofed kitchen.

There was a stone close to the door, thus the place I used to sit while facing those three figures of stones, which carry my pot to cook my food every day. "You poor stones, why can't you run away from being burned by my fire wood every day?" I questioned them.

Nature can speak, but the question came back to me. In that same moment, I recalled the events, which happened to my life. This was not a dream but the reality. There are situations in life when we conclude that the only option is to run away instead of facing them.

The familiars' of yesterday should not bring us to see the possibilities of tomorrow as un attainable and the philosophy going on that we can't make it in the mist of all the fires around should give us the muscle to go on do what our today has not done and when our weakest part rises, the strongest part must overcome.

I was so stupid to question those stones to run away from the fire it faces every day. It was like taking away gold from the fire, it would not be gold anymore. Those stones saved their nature and thus the same with human nature. We are called to save the world in the midst of challenges.

Those stones were saving its natural responsibility but like many of us, we think it is not right, its natural character is to save against the fire, and the human nature is created to save more than that. The ability to survive against great challenges we think the only option is to run away was placed in every human.

I was all alone facing those stones in that empty roofed kitchen. The pain from my broken finger was so heavy. The day before I was at the hospital and that corrupt doctor was the one who plaster my hand after Mafie gave him something and the day before yesterday we were there again but that black assistant refused to attend to us he said time was over he couldn't gave us any attention because we had not what he need.

He had no idea of how much pain I was feeling. I was not the only one turned back. There was with me in the group of many patients. Grandfathers and children so tired. How can you turn back the patients because of money, which will go to your pockets? They are big doctors doing this in public hospitals and they do not pity the poor. "Go and die or seek the way to survive."

If you want to know how much serious one is in his plans, discourage him fist and if he continues then he knows what he is doing and you cannot stop him anymore.

When Mafie and I had nothing to offer ourselves on the table, there was nothing to worry as long as it was the rainy season. If we had flour and cooking oil, it was fine, I could go to the fields of people nearby to seek for some natural vegetables, which grow when the rain falls. I could mix five types of these vegetables and cook them. It made a nice mill with stiff porridge. Mafie wondered where I learned these and some vegetables he has never eaten them before.

He was amazed many times, on how I cop up with the situation especially on the days when we had nothing. Sometimes it could seem impossible to have a mill but when he comes back he could wonder how possible that I have cooked and where did I get it. I used dry leaves and glasses to cook when we had no firewood.

Gathering those dry leaves and glasses was the most impossible thing he never dreamt I could do. Mafie wondered where and how did I got such a strength and boldness to stand in such a hard situation.

To him, I went as far as a soldier. He looked at me; many young people of my age already had marriages and others seem to be far in their dreams achievements. I was 28 by that time but I seem not to be in hurry.

Some of my friends had good jobs and were happy but Mafie had no idea about happiness. I do not rush for something in order to find happiness for even mad people knows how to be happy they open in the rich man's dustbin while laughing.

And if so, then the rich could not cry with all the dollars in the bank. I must go beyond happiness and thus to find my identity because in my identity there are colors of life, the style of living and the freedom of myself.

I was not to board that bus of life, which everybody rushes to. It was all nothing to me when I penetrate in their footsteps the missing of their identity for every achievement is anything when one has not laid the foundation of his identity, which can introduce him to the generations to come. A man who has his foundations of his identity lives for generations and does not die in his generation alone. These are men whose the coming generations will seek to know and learn from and set a new footsteps at the end of the road.

If you live more than thirty years and still do the same things then you have not learned anything in this life, which could change your prospective. One has to grow up to his identity then he can differentiate himself among the wise and the fools. I have come across friends who have wives and children but still childish. They think, live and dream as in the teens. I have come to learn that we do not need to grow up but we need to mature.

Still begging money from friends, talking nonsense and many times walk around without doing anything.beg money from friends in order to develop yourself and not for drinking. Many African nations are asking for donor funds and pass huge amount of nation budget at the parliament for their own profits they do nothing with those money except of having expensive life across Africa.

They take their leave to enjoy themselves in the hotels of America and Dubai instead of paying the same money to their local hotels and that money would be used locally, but they receive donor funds from America use it in the way they want and go fly to America where the funds came from and use it there.

The first thing they do when they come into power is to know the nation's money channels so that they know where to reduce the amount and put the other part into their secret personal accounts. True politics is not stealing from poor people nor taking advantages over the weak. Is not gathering to one's self the national riches nor looking down on the oppressed, true politics is to meet people's needs and having a nation as the first goal.

THE DIRTY ROOM.

I moved from Mafie after two solid years of living with him and I decide to be alone. One woman called Margret connected me to a man called John who was running his school but had a problem of administration. He had the money to manage the school but the management was so poor. It was a good luck to me.

For the first seven months, I had all I needed on my table. John's wife was keeping chickens for slaughtering she had tenders to supply the chickens, and whenever she slaughters' she could not forget to bring one for me twice a week. Eating that complete roosted chicken alone was another paradise to me where there are no sorrows as it is said, that every dog has its day, I at least forgot the vegetables from Mafie.

Since my arrival to help run the school, everything changed and the academic and the management went beyond excellent. Things changed when John came to hit a pedestrian with his car when the man died on the sport. John was taken to jail and when he came out he had lost a lot and now he had the time to follow up the case

When he come out life was not the same, he was suffering from the psychological attack. He had many debts from people and most of them were demanding their money his enemies tried all their best to use their philosophy that the government should take away his tourism company license his wife was now the in change of the family and thus when I learned that a man who has a strong wife is most blessed.

Their kinds were spelled out from the school because they lacked the school fees. This caused the bad effect to the school I was running because many needs were now scares. John came one day with the news that he wants the school to be closed because he could not move on anymore.

I did not agree with him and I told him not to do that, give me time, I told him. He lastly took my idea to wait for a change.

I took one classroom and make it my bedroom because I had to be close to monitor everything since I was the one depended on. And thus, another page of my book was opened. Since I knew, I would not live in that room forever I did not trouble myself to make it fancy. I created the environment, which would force me to concentrate on my writings.

I had no habit of sleeping at night, I spent many hours on that plastic chair writing my books and when I got tired I lay myself on the floor I could put some of my clothes down fist to avoid that coldness and I become the mosquitoes food. I could not care sometimes about those hungry mosquitoes, when I see that they trouble me too much, I could stay myself silent and never trouble myself to chase after them. I could let them to suck me as much blood as they wanted so that when they are full they stop to whisper for food in my ears.

In the morning I could find them holding against the walls with their big stomachs full of my blood felling to fly for their lives I could revenge them; Phaaa! I hit one with my hand splashing blood on my hands.

In Africa and many parts of the world when a young man is free to lead his life alone and he has a lonely bedroom, the next thing he dreamed to do with that room is snatch girls many tights and lock them there and temptations for girls increases on such moments.

Sleeping on that floor kept my mind from temptations of girls. I was handsome, am handsome and I will be handsome even on my dearth and those girls who climbs the praying mountains to pray for their future husbands they seek for handsome young men in the area and then they go before God and ask him to give them that man and then they come to start to walk around you believing God would answer their lust for handsome men. 'Get out!'

I had many of them around me but they all came to the wrong answer. Not everything is spiritual sometimes life goes by chance and I must say that many of them with those long prayers they spent, they do not find the men they wanted and they are not even happy in their marriages because they asked wrongly.

I kept my room as dirty as a rat. James my neighbor's young man was as dirty as me so we make great team of two. He kept me company many times eating my food without any contribution.

I did not like him when he gets drunk. He came demanding my food when his mother kept him away from her food when he gets drunk. I just endured with him for his immaturity but little by little he started to change and we become good friends. I come to learn that nothing shall come perfect in our hands but there is power in our hands to make them imperfect perfect. As I write, he is now a father of two kinds and no more drinking.

To be cruel on others is one of the effects we inherited from slavery. In many African societies you will trace the spirit of mastership for masters never care how others feels masters live to make themselves happy and put themselves in front many times.

I have experienced many people in my life and in many sectors who pretends to be good people while in their characters' there are hidden swords.

There are some bad behaviors we inherited from slavery, which I hated so much. Most Africans gets angry where they ought to laugh and laugh where they ought to cry. They smile where they ought to be sorrowful and they condemn and judge when they must teach and instruct and lead. They discourage where they ought to encourage. They react, judge everything wrong without taking time to think, and reason to see if there is something helpful in it.

They stand on someone's opportunities and bad enough preventing a close friend from being successful and worse enough dancing for someone's fall. They calls you a good person and cast all good recommendations about you in front of others but when you turn your back they calls you a donkey.

And many families pretends to love each other in front of visitors, when a visitor comes a man and a woman sits together on that sofa so cross while they know in their hearts that they spent the long day without talking to each other and when a visitor turns back they began to exchange words and show their angry faces against each other. The moment where a wife becomes a man and a man becomes a wife.

There are solitary tears flowing in many house girls, she is slapped by that masters wife in the morning because of that little mistake and spent the day without given food to eat and upon given the food the masters wife says many abusive words until the appetite for it gets lost, she just eat for her stomach and not for her heart. And in the afternoon, the boss himself comes to sleep with her deceiving his wife that he is going home for lunch while he is going to play with that little girl without her willingness, never ashamed with all that his big stomachs like a pregnant elephant.

What a pity boss is you, you have given her pregnant five times and in all those times you took her in your car telling your wife that you are taking her to town for shopping while you drive her to the hospital to abort and in the fifth time that your doctor stupid like you told you that her womb had been destroyed and she will not be able to bare kinds anymore but foolish as you are you didn't tell her.

She moved from you a man loved her to make a family but years have passed without getting pregnant and there is no peace with her man and friends scorn at her while you did it all. Destroying other peoples future is the most thing I hate in life. You pity boss you did the same with your secretary but today you have met me the prostitute of truth.

You are the most respected man in the society but now you have to tell me what made you to run from your beautiful wife and come to me this night. That your wife has everything a woman has to have. Big shining eyes, high hips, and big legs like a football player. Don't you love her flapping checks like a rat? Answer me, don't you love her?

Am the prostitute of truth and I do not sleep around with foolish men. You are a dad at your home and a boss at your office and in your nation they call you a leader and at your religion they calls you a good man and you come to me and I'm more than a boss anyone who comes to me comes to another world with different rules the world which stands not on any human philosophy but the truth in the darkness.

You love the darkness isn't it? We are in this room but you do not want the lights on because you do not want to be seen. I like the dark too because in it is when I come to know what happens in this world.

Now I must tell you that I will never stop to be a prostitute and I will never stop to love the darkness because thus where I found the secrets. My nakedness does me good and when you point, your fingers on my nakedness be careful because I know more than you. Some men the world thinks are strong are the foolish ones when your eyes can have a chance to meet them in the dark.

Men surround us and women who pretend to live in the light. Politicians and religious leaders, celebrities and worthy young men who live in the light but does everything in the dark.

It's not of a surprise anymore to see a pastor going around with women of his own church, not a surprise to hear that smart politicians respected by the society is a corrupt one and other peoples riches depends on innocent peoples suffering and taking advantage over weak woman in the night has become the life style of many well known men in our society.

THE GREATEST LESSON FROM COVID 19

Perhaps the future generation will have to question what was the worst tragedy ever happened to man in the 21st century; no doubt that in the worlds libraries there shall be piles of books written about Covid 19 the Corona virus which killed more than five million people by book(the number might change) in the the time I was finishing to write this world . But the most surprising story will be how the Africans survived? Since the days of the explorers and the missionaries, all what was reported about Africa in the European nations was that Africa is a trash of diseases and that survival would take a risk and a sacrifice.

The world expected more deaths in Africa than anywhere else in the world because it has been proved for generations that disease belongs to the poor and not the poor of anywhere else but the poor of Africa. I have explained more in my book called "Africa Shall Live."

But what is the greatest lesson the world has learned in 21st century? The greatest lesson the world has learned from the Covid 19 is to know that the knowledge for survival we have learned for the past decades is not enough for our present and the future human survival.

Man must know that the discoveries and the scientific knowledge that has been written and the philosophy which has been guiding man to live and pass the testing times is not enough for the present and the future survival.

Doctors completes four years undergraduate along with four years in medical school and three to seven years in residency program to learn the specialty they chose to pursue. In other words, it takes between 10 to 14 years to become a fully licensed doctor. Philosophers take 5 to 7 years of study about philosophy after completion of their college degree including 2 to 3 years of course work. So we can say it takes almost 10 years for philosophy study. To become a scientist it takes 4 years for college, 5 years for a doctorate, and 3 years for post doctorate research, which is 12 years of study for one to become a professor in science.

How do you imagine that many years of study come to be nothing in just a day of Covid 19! 14 years of studying to be a professional doctor did not give man a solution for survival. Thousands of people died in the midst of professional scientists with high and updated technology.

The world has lived to prepare for the things, which are present but has no idea for the unknown comings, which the conclusion is that man is still limited in the knowledge of survival. Something must be done where in the future thousands shall not die and the vast majority of men shall not lose jobs and if it happens again to lose jobs, they will not go back home and stay idol. I mean great discoveries where men shall not need a lockdown to survive.

Man should not live to think that his professionalism is enough for the survival of the dark days coming ahead of the world and the government accounts are not enough to save the lives. Plans and strategies are needed which just comes from the human minds and not from any experience and those who question about God as the last hope for man's survival must re think again but God himself uses people. The Covid 19 Corona virus shock the world to the extent that in the worlds history for the first time in 21st century the world leaders confessed that God alone can bring us to the survival and how can I forget president John Joseph Pombe Magufuli the republic of Tanzania who declared the three days of national prayer, and gets what? It worked.

While other nations were locked up, Tanzania was open and all was going as usual as if Corona virus does not exist. Where can a human race find its refuge when the human philosophy declines?

We are living in the times of great invention though technology and science and the future technology is awesome than what we see now and I wish to live those days coming ahead. The flying cars, flying buses, amazing speed electric trains, robots on both the military and the industry and everywhere but the enemies of our society like the climate change, terrorist, viruses and bacteria's, war, hate, selfishness, power control, selfish politics, shall one day make the dream of the world to nothing for Covid 19 has left us with such a big lesson.

But my massage to the future and the days to come is that no matter what type of technology shall exist, the thing is one that the human race needs to survive in the times of crisis. No matter how sweet life shall be, there is no sweetness when one wakes up one day to find that all televisions announces about the unknown disease without cure.

No sweetness waking up one day to see that Hiroshima and Nagasaki have been bombed with atomic boom and the generations of the survivals will have to face its consequences for decades. Don't use technologies to kill fellow human being use it to at list give simplicity to human living instead?

The fear and the terror, which has faced the world on Covid 19, should give strength to the times of testing which shall fall upon the world in the future that man was given one possibility and thus overcoming the obstacles when there is a possibility. Not everybody shall die in the testing times; others shall live even if it be one person left among the millions the secret of life is that nature preserves its kind that there should never lack the seed to multiply after the testing times has reduced the population of creation.

The industries, which make gun weapons, cannot do business without a profit. They must sell their weapons to make money in the whole world which invent gun weapons and other chemical weapons for business. The truth of the matter is that they must sell and continue to invent better weapons and the time to test those weapons to see how destructive and effective they are, they must test them where people are available as an advertisement to the weapon buyers Everything happens around our time now is all about business.

The chemist must sell their newly discovered invasion across the globe and the business can't work if some viruses will not be created to affect millions of people around the world and the rich men will not invest in the world organizations of hearth, and science laboratories where billions of money are invested just to test some work of created viruses and bacteria and some of our people announced to get lost or caught by the unknown people are taken as part of virus test in their experimental laboratories. Science kills hundreds of people in order to heal thousands of people.

DESTINY ON TRIAL

Destiny has never been easy and never shall it be neither. Africa lost almost 2.4 million of her people as slaves and the number is said to be higher because millions died on seasoning camps as they wait for the voyage and others died during the transportation on the sea to America and Europe for sell. Millions died in civil wars, caused by the political instability.

But the truth is that life has many secrets and some bad events, which happen in our lives, are the very way to take us to our destiny. There will be the bloodshed on the way, betrayals and tears. We will be strangers and oppressed by the known and the unknown people yes rejected by the most loved ones the very same we gave our trust and hearts. Sometimes the world will turn against us without a cause and taken advantage innocently.

And sometimes-bad staff happens in our lives one after another to the extent that we lost to trust anybody. We become like a virgin who in the way of persuading a good man ends up in bad hands and at the end concludes that all men are liars and that no man can be trusted and if that was true then we couldn't read and sang about Romeo and Juliet. Concluding that all things happens in this world are fake is not true, the real thing is that you have not met that real thing yet!

One day in 2011 when I was living in Tanzania in the Kilimanjaro Airport houses area, I tried to stop cars, which were coming from the Airport. Because Tanzania is a hospitable country, you can stop a motorcycle or a car to give you a lift when you are in a hurry in the areas where there are no public busses' so I stand to stop one to take me up.

I tried to stop almost twelve cars but none stopped but the thirteenth one stopped and amazingly drives me to the point of my journey than I expected. It was a nice car not just a car.

I would be wrong to conclude that all car owners are selfish before I had not waited enough until to the number I had not known. When the first passed be by I thought the second one would pick me up and it goes like that waiting the numbers of car one after another until my hope for the next number comes though I had now lost the hope to all car owner that someone would pick me up.

It was the day I come to learn the greatest lesson in life that no matter how many men have been bad to us but good people still exist and are out there! We are living in the times where men have lost hope in humanity because everything around seem to be rotten. Our national leaders have discouraged us and nothing good is expected from our politicians! The evidence is seen during the general elections that many do not want to go to vote because they think it would be the same. And some few unfaithful religious men and women have caused all religious men to look like fishes having one smell. The world fears to put young men in front positions because they fear they will scatter everything in luxury life. Beautiful young women fear to get marriage life because faithfulness has lost its way.

I come to learn that we do not choose destiny but that destiny choose us and when destiny chooses you it will take you to the ways and directions, you will not want. Some people's destiny will take them through the valleys of the shadow of death where life and dearth say hello to each other. Destiny has its own ways you cannot lead it; it leads you.

Because destiny was what chose me and was what leads me I forgot all the pain, I forgive all who betrayed me while they call themselves friends and brothers and to some I even tried to put my trust and call them fathers and mothers. It was not you it was destiny and you were part of the destiny. I myself wanting forgiveness from friends and family who by being in need of me I was not there when they need me and I know I caused much tears to many innocent eyes, I know I caused pain and sorrow to many hearts but it wasn't me it was destiny .

I didn't gave the results of expectation expected but the truth of life is that not everybody was chosen for a certain task and there are some missions which are a must to be carried out under the sun and if they are a must by the heavens then those who are chosen have no choice because their everything is removed away from their eyes and are left without a choice.

Something's happens as a mystery to our lives until another time when we come to be reveled of why it happens like that. The bad side of life you do not like to pass through is what produces you. And sometimes destiny will not rest in you until it finds a place to conceive what is in you. And its not usual to find the kings born in the palace.

So it's about nobody around, nobody is to be blamed, and in all that I went through good or bad was part of fulfilling my life destiny. Now what remains is one; “moving on”.

Now I know it wasn’t me but destiny in trial pushing me through itself.

7

9

THE DECLINE OF HUMAN PHILOSOPHY

THE DECLINE OF HUMAN PHILOSOPHY

THE DECLINE OF HUMAN PHILOSOPHY

THE DECLINE OF HUMAN PHILOSOPHY

THE DECLINE OF HUMAN PHILOSOPHY

THE DECLINE OF HUMAN PHILOSOPHY

www.ingramcontent.com/pod-product-compliance
Lightning Source LLC
LaVergne TN
LVHW012054160826
845678LV00014B/2818

* 9 7 9 8 8 4 1 9 9 2 4 0 0 *